From GOD through Moses to YOU

VOLUME 2
EXODUS / SHEMOT

"We are living in exciting times when the Spirit of the Living God is awakening Christians and Jews to the Jewishness of Jesus and the Hebraic roots of Christianity. After centuries of being separated by the traditions of men, the "people of the Book" are reexamining the Book of Books in its cultural context. This has caused both Christians and Jews to realize that when we strip our respective faith of the traditions of men, we have the same faith in the covenant God of history and His Messiah. I appreciate this book Allen has written that contributes to this critical understanding."

Dr. Richard Booker, Author of 40 books
Teacher of the Word of God
Speaker at Feast of Tabernacles,
Jerusalem, Israel *(every year)*

From GOD through Moses to YOU

VOLUME 2
EXODUS / SHEMOT

Written by
Allen C. Ranney Th.D

A BOLD TRUTH Publication
Christian Literature & Artwork

From GOD through Moses to YOU
Volume 2 EXODUS / SHEMOT
Copyright © 2019 Allen C. Ranney
ISBN 13: 978-1-949993-10-3

FIRST EDITION
⏺

Jew and Gentile Ministries
P.O. Box 1981
Sapulpa, OK 74066
www.jewandgentileministries.org

Bold Truth Publishing
606 W. 41st, Ste. 4
Sand Springs, Oklahoma 74063
www.BoldTruthPublishing.com
boldtruthbooks@yahoo.com

08 19   10 9 8 7 6 5 4 3 2 1

Permissions

Interlinear Bible, the, Hendrickson publishing, 2006

The Strong's Complete Dictionary of Bible Words (Nashville, TN: Thomas Nelson publishing, 1996

Dedication

It is with immense pleasure that I dedicate this work to Karen, my loving wife, whose unwavering faith in God, her pursuit of holiness, her scriptural knowledge and her steadfast love for me has made teaching Torah and writing "From GOD through Moses to YOU" such a joy.

Table of Contents

Contents

Endorsements

"This book will serve as a magnificent resource to explore in depth meanings for Hebrew and Messianic studies. There is a simple, yet profound way that brings understanding to the Hebrew words and when combined with Scripture brings incredible understanding for the reader. This is a must for every library for students of the Word and Hebrew study."

> – *Drs. Jerry & Sherill Piscopo*
> Destiny Christian University
> Chancellors & Founders

~

"My wife and I enjoy so much these Messianic Torah Parashah. The quotes in Hebrew give me a chance every day to practice my basic Biblical reading skills. Though we are not Jewish, we understand that the Lord speaks through His Holy Word. Thank you for helping people to hear His Voice through your book 'From God Through Moses To You'"

> – *Pastor John Denson*
> President Shalom Ministry

~

"We thank G-d for Dr. Ranney, for his work draws from the heart of G-d the true meaning of the Scriptures from the Bereshiit Genesis to the Amen of the Revelation to give a better understanding of the unity of the 1st Covenant, OT, and the Brit Hadassah, NT. That will bridge the Jewish people and non-Jewish through the plan of G-d together. Dr. Allen Ranney has brought therefore a magnificent tool to break down the walls of partition that were brought through the historical events and the teachings of doctrines.

"Therefore, this book is meant to reach churches, organizations, schools, educational institutes, etc. and people from every walk of life to be building bridges of shalom peace and unity of faith in G-d, who is Triune echad for all."

> – *Rabbi Dr. Avraham and Dr. Irmeli Libertus*
> Founders and the Senior Leaders, Calvary Messianic Congregation; Founders, International Bible University and Messianic Institute; Founders, Hebrew Language and Culture School & Jerusalem Dancers; Libertus Global Ministries

~

"Dr. Ranney has produced a work that has the potential to fulfill the life-long desire of the Apostle Paul, the most zealous Jew that ever lived. Despite being called to be the Apostle to the Gentiles, Paul's burning desire was for both groups to be united (Romans 10:1). With From God, Through Moses, to You, those on both sides, if they will read it with an open-mind and a spirit of humility, can make Paul's desire for this unity come to fruition."

> – *Jack Miner*
> Christian Editing and Publishing

Acknowledgments

First, I would like to thank my wife, Karen, for being the loving, praying, supporting, beautiful woman that she is. She has always encouraged me to draw closer to our Lord Yeshua, that He should lead and guide me.

Secondly, I will mention Calvary Messianic congregation and I.B.U./I.M.I. where I was privileged to teach Torah and embrace the Messianic root of our faith.

I would like to thank Rabbi Abraham Libertus and Dr. Irmeli Libertus, for their excellence in teaching.

I would like to thank Kevin Day, administrator at Life Gate Freedom Recovery Ranch and my ministerial partner there, Charles Ballard. Together we have battled the drug addiction and alcoholism in the men that received treatment there, these past nine years.

Also, I would like to acknowledge my editor and publisher Aaron Jones, for encouraging me to write another book.

And last I would like to thank my father and mother for instilling in me the foundational faith at an early age, that in my old age I shall not depart from.

Acknowledgments

Introduction

"From God, Through Moses, To You" is a compilation of 3½ years of teaching Torah at the largest Messianic assembly in Tulsa, Oklahoma.

Torah teaching consists of reading, then studying so you can prepare a lesson. Something wonderful happens every time you read Torah. As you learn Torah, the Holy Spirit will give you something; revelation, insight, knowledge, something new, something special just for you. I wouldn't say this had I not experienced time after time, the Holy Spirit giving me a little nugget of wisdom from the Word of God. Sometimes that little nugget is a personal revelation that I keep and cherish, but most often it's a word of knowledge that begs to be shared with the whole world. That's what you will find in the text of this book, the nuggets and words of knowledge which I have been given to share with you.

1 Corinthians 2:9-10 reads, "But it is written: 'Eye has not seen, nor ear heard, nor have entered into the heart of man the things which God has prepared for those who love Him.' But God has revealed them to us through His Spirit. For the Spirit searches all things, yes the deep things of God".

There is a dual-purpose to this book. One, to bring the Messianic perspective into the Jewish community. Two, to bring the Jewish perspective to the Christian Church which has, in many cases, forsaken the Old Testament, choosing to focus almost exclusively on the New Testament, thereby losing so much of the foundational wisdom God has put in the Bible. Many Christians today struggle to understand the Old Testament and many Jews today do not understand the New Testament. One aim of this book is to bring together the Old Testament and the New Testament in a comprehensive form that Jews and Gentiles alike can relate to.

In these Torah studies, the Holy Spirit uses words, specifically the titles of the weekly portions, the Parashah, as a focus for the lesson itself to teach us the spiritual truths He wants us to understand. God uses the unction and urgings of the Spirit in us because Adam lost that perfect personal relationship with Him through sin. In our sinful condition, we can no longer speak with God face-to-face for a complete understanding of His thoughts and intents. We now perceive things through the Holy Spirit's movement in ourselves as we cannot perceive the things of God in a pure physical sense as did Adam. We get word pictures, snapshots, brief video clips or parts, but not the full work of what God is doing on this earth.

Unfortunately, Western civilization (Christian) has misunderstood or even corrupted those word pictures God is trying to show us in Torah. Christians have done this by trying to apply modern Western thought to a book written from a Semitic perspective to a Semitic audience. Thankfully, we have the words of Yeshua Messiah in the New Testament to clarify most of Torah for the Gentile mind.

When we apply the lessons and words learned in the Gospels to the lessons and words of the Torah, the Scriptures come alive in both their Jewish and Gentile cultural contexts. Then the word pictures that the Holy Spirit paints for us stand out in bold color on the canvas. Yes, the Torah is a masterpiece that is timeless in context, information, thought and intent, and is available to Jews and Gentile alike for personal revelation and interpretation; but it comes with a great responsibility to deliver God's Word without muddying it with our own shortsightedness and prejudices. We are warned in James 3:1, "My brother, let not many of you become teachers knowing that we shall receive a stricter judgment." Amen.

Each chapter in this book is arranged with a portion title introduction and an overview of the portion's biblical texts. I suggest a thorough reading of the weekly Torah Portion before reading this book, however, this book is comprehensive on its own, as some people are pressed for time, or the thought of having to read 6 to 10 chapters before actually reading from another book might be too much.

One reason to read the whole Torah Portion, Haftarah or Prophet's Portion, and suggested Gospel reading first is because it is the inspired Word of God and not the work of a man. Another reason is that the Holy Spirit reveals from Scripture that which the Lord has for you personally.

This book is what I feel the Spirit has led me to write. I have given it to the Lord on the Brazen Altar as an offering, a sweet savor unto Him; and He blessed me with the opportunity to teach Torah. Most of all, He blessed me with personal spiritual insight I would not have gained otherwise. I pray Shad-dai Melach Ha Olam bless you in kind.

– Allen Ranney Th.D
Jew and Gentile Ministries
jewandgentileministries.org

Prayer

It is a Hebrew tradition to pray immediately after waking in the mornings and continually throughout the day. There are prayers for the family, for moral strength, on starting a journey, prayers for Israel, prayers for the home, prayer for rain, prayer for meals, afternoon prayers and evening prayers. There are prayers for every occasion, Shabbat, all the feasts and prayers for the new moon and more!

I love to pray, it is a time of communion and communication between Yeshua Messiah and myself. I will not be legalistic about prayer though. I pray for and about everything, especially before reading from the Word of God. I would like to share one of the prayers I pray before and after reading Torah.

A prayer before reading Torah

Baruch atah Adonai Elohim, Melech Olam, asher bachar min kol ha'goyim v'natan l'anu Torah. Baruch atah Yeshua nathan ha'Torah. Amen.

Bless You Lord God, King everlasting, Who chose us from all the nations and gave us Torah. Blessed are You Yeshua, giver of the Torah. Amen.

A prayer after reading Torah

Baruch atah Adonai Elohim, Melech Olam, atah nathan anu eth Torah emet v'nata chay olam b'qerebnu. Baruch atah Yeshua, nathanu ha'Torah. Amen.

Bless you Lord God, King everlasting, You gave us Your Torah of truth and planted life everlasting in our midst. Bless You Yeshua, giver of the Torah. Amen.

From GOD through Moses to YOU

Shemot

"names"

Exodus 1:1-6:1
Isaiah 27:6-28:13, 29:22-23
Luke 5:12-39

This Torah study titled "Shemot" in Hebrew means "names." The names of the children of Israel, Jacob's twelve sons, who were the founders of the tribes of Israel that grew into the nation of Israel: Reuben, Simeon, Levi, Judah, Issachar, Zebulun, Dan, Naphtali, Gad, Asher, Joseph and Benjamin. The extraordinary growth of the family of promise in Egypt is a great miracle. Evidence of God's blessings and God's hand in this miracle are recorded throughout the book of Exodus.

A miracle is a less common way of God working. It is done to arouse people's surprise, awe or amazement in such a way that God bears witness of Himself in and through signs, wonders and marvels.

Additional Scripture

Isaiah 35:1-2   Luke 12:27
Ezekiel 36:34-36   Romans 10:8-13
Matthew 6:28   Mark 16:15-18

From GOD through Moses to YOU

This week's Torah Portion (Parashat #6557) is in Exodus 1:1-6:1 and is titled "Shemot #8034" in Hebrew and means "names."

Exodus 1:1-22 records Israel's suffering in Egypt.

Exodus 2:1-10 records the birth of Moses.

Exodus 2:11-25 records Moses fleeing to Midian.

Exodus 3:1-22 records the miracle of the burning bush.

Exodus 4:1 records miraculous signs for Pharaoh.

Exodus 5:1 records Moses' first encounter with Pharaoh.

Exodus 5:22-6:1 records Israel's deliverance is assured by God.

The Haftarah or Prophets' Portion is in Isaiah 27:6-28:13, 29:22-23

Isaiah 27:6 records Israel shall blossom and bud.

Isaiah 28:1-13 records warnings to Ephraim and Jerusalem.

Isaiah 29:22-23 records Jacob shall not be ashamed.

The Gospel Portion is in Luke 5:12-39

Luke 5:12 records a leper is cleansed.

Luke 5:16- 39 records a paralytic is healed, and Matthew is called.

Shemot "names"

Torah Portion
Exodus 1:1-6:1

Exodus 1:1 (Interlinear Bible) reads, "And these were the "Shemot #8034", "names" of the sons of Israel who came into Egypt with Jacob; they each one came in with his house."

This is where we get the title for this week's Torah Portion. "Shemot" in Hebrew means "names," specifically the names of Jacob's (Israel's) 12 children, who are the founders of the tribes of Israel that grew into the nation of Israel. Reuben, Simeon, Levi, Judah, Issachar, Zebulun, Dan, Naphtali, Gad, Asher, Joseph and Benjamin. The extraordinary growth of the family of promise in Egypt is a great miracle, and evidence of God's blessing and God's hand in this miracle are recorded throughout the book of Exodus.

"Now there arose a new king over Egypt, who did not know Joseph. And he said to his people, "look, the people of the children of Israel are more and mightier than we; come, let us deal shrewdly with them, lest they multiply, and it happen, in the event of war, that they also join our enemies and fight against us, and so go up out of the land." Therefore, they set taskmasters over them to afflict them with their burdens, and they built for Pharaoh supply cities, Pithom, and Raamses. But the more they afflicted them, the more they multiplied and grew. And they were in dread of the children of Israel. So the Egyptians made the children of Israel serve with rigor. And they made their lives bitter with hard bondage – in mortar, in brick, and in all manner of service in the field. All their service in which they made them serve with rigor." (Exodus 1:8-14)

From GOD through Moses to YOU

Verse 12 reads "but the more they afflicted them, the more they multiplied and grew." For 400 years, no matter the situation, the people of God multiplied.... Miracle.

"Then the king of Egypt spoke to the Hebrew midwives, of whom the name of one was Shiphrah and the name of the other was Puah; and he said, "when you do the duties of a midwife for the Hebrew women, and see them on the birth stools, if it is a son, then you shall kill him; but if it is a daughter, then she shall live." But the midwives feared God and did not do as the king of Egypt commanded them, but saved the male children live." Exodus 1:20-22 reads, "therefore God dealt well with the midwives, and the people multiplied and grew very mighty, and so it was, because the midwives feared God, that He provided households for them. So Pharaoh commanded all his people, saying, "every son who is born you shall cast into the river, and every daughter you shall save alive." (Exodus 1:15-27)

It's interesting to note that the king of Egypt's name is not recorded here, but the "Shemot" names of the two God-fearing midwives are, Shiphrah and Puah.

"Shiphrah #8236" in Hebrew means "beautiful one," beautiful like how the dew glistens in the morning sun.

"Puah #6312" in Hebrew means "splendid one," splendid like the light that glistens off jewels.

Two shining examples of God fearing women. Exodus 1:18 tells of Pharaoh calling for these two midwives and asking them why they didn't do as he ordered. In ancient times, if you didn't do as the king said, that was grounds for execution or at least imprisonment. But God did not just save the midwives, He provided households for them…. Miracle.

Exodus 2:1-10 records Moses' birth to a man and wife of the house of Levi

"And she hid him for three months, but when she could hide him no more she built an ark of bullrushes for him and laid it in the reeds by the river bank and his sister stood afar off to know what would become of him and it happened that Pharaoh's daughter came down to the river to bathe and when she saw the ark among the reeds she sent her maid to get it. Then his sister said to Pharaoh's daughter, "shall I go and call a nurse for you from the Hebrew women, that she may nurse the child for you?" And Pharaoh's daughter said to her, "go." So the maiden went and called the child's mother. Then Pharaoh's daughter said to her, "take this child away and nurse him for me, and I will give you your wages." So the woman took the child and nursed him. And the child grew, and she brought him to Pharaoh's daughter, and he became her son. So she called his name Moses #4822, saying, "because I drew him out of the water."

The Nile River was full of crocodiles and yet the daughter of Pharaoh finds the Hebrew child, and in direct defiance of her father's decree to kill all the male Hebrew children, she decides to keep him and raise him as her own …Miracle.

Exodus 2:11-15 NKJV reads, "One day, when Moshe was a grown man, he went out to visit his kinsman; and he watched them struggling at forced labor. He saw an Egyptian strike

From GOD through Moses to YOU

a Hebrew, one of his kinsman. He looked this way and that; and when he saw that no one was around, he killed the Egyptian and hid his body in the sand."

Of course, the murder, is found out and Moses has to escape from Egypt to the land of Midian. Midian just happened to be a son of Abraham by Keturah,

So the priest of Midian "Reuel" is a direct descendent of Abraham. "Reuel #7467" in Hebrew means "friend of God. So, Moses escapes a sure death sentence in Egypt and finds a "friend of God" in Midian…. Miracle.

"Now Moses was tending the flock of Jethro (#3503 Jethro meaning his preeminence or his excellence) the priest of Midian and Moses' father-in-law (Jethro is called Reuel in Exodus 2:18, which means friend of God, Reuel seems to have been his personal name, and Jethro, his excellence, to have been his honorary title) and he led the flock to the back of the desert, and came to Horeb, the mountain of God. And the Angel of the Lord appeared to him in a flame of fire from the midst of a bush. So he looked, and behold, the bush was burning with fire, but the bush was not consumed. Then Moses said, "I will now turn aside to see this great sight, why the bush does not burn." So when the Lord saw that he turned aside to look, God called to him from the midst of the bush and said, "Moses, Moses!" And he said, "here I am." Then He said, "do not draw near this place. Take your sandals off your feet, for the place where you stand is holy ground. "Moreover He said, "I am the God of your father – the God of Abraham, the God of Isaac, and the God of Jacob." And Moses hid his face, for he was afraid to look upon God." (Exodus 3:1-6)

Burning bush? Not consumed by the fire?.... Miracle. God speaking from the midst of the burning bush… Miracle.

Warning! Anytime a man or woman tries to explain God's miracles in this earth by likening them to some natural phenomena, occurrence or event, in essence they are cheapening God's Word and works. They try to make the supernatural, miraculous works of God as common as dirt. The bush is not consumed by the Holy fire of God… Miracle… God speaking from the midst of the burning bush… Miracle…it cannot be said enough!

Exodus 3:14 (Interlinear Bible) reads, "and God said to Moses "I AM" that I AM; and He said, you shall say this to the sons of Israel, I AM has sent me to you."

I "AM" #1961 "Hayah" in Hebrew is translated here as "I AM" but it is also translated as "been, came, exists, am, went and went on continually." Our God is introducing Himself to Moses and the children of Israel as the Ever Existent One, Amen! And He goes on to say in Exodus 3:15b, "this is My Name #8034 Forever #5769", "Ha Shem L'olam" and this is My "Zekar #2142", "Memorial, name, title to all generations." Amen. God is our Father; we are invited to come into His presence, boldly calling upon Him.

Romans 8:15 reads, "for you did not receive the spirit of bondage again to fear, but you received the Spirit of adoption by whom we cry out, "Abba, Father." The Spirit Himself bears witness with our spirit that we are children of God."

"Let us therefore come boldly to the throne of grace, that we may obtain mercy and find grace to help in time of need." (Hebrews 4:16)

Amen. God wants us to call on Him by His personal "Shemot" names, God wants to have a personal relationship with us" .... Miracle.

Exodus 4 records that Moses was given miraculous signs to show in Pharaoh's court.

The rod, probably a shepherd's crook, turns into a snake and back again.... Miracle.

Moses' hand turned leprous white and back again.... Miracle.

Exodus 5:1-6 records Moses' first encounter with Pharaoh.

"Afterward Moses and Aaron went in and told Pharaoh, "Thus says the Lord God of Israel: "let My people go, that they may hold a feast to Me in the wilderness." And Pharaoh said, "who is the Lord, that I should obey His voice to let Israel go? I do not know the Lord, nor will I let Israel go." (Exodus 5:1)

This first meeting between Moses and Pharaoh did not go well according to the recollections of man. Pharaoh's heart was hard and the Lord used that to fulfill all the plans He had for His chosen people Israel.

Miracle after miracle, two men, Moses and Aaron, one a

wanted murderer, the other, a slave and shepherd, standing before the Pharaoh, king of Egypt, defying him, making demands of him, not honoring him, but reverencing another "Shem" name in his presence, disrespecting him, yet they lived.... Miracle!!!

Haftarah Portion
Isaiah 27:6-28, 29:22-23

"Those who come He shall cause to take root in Jacob; Israel shall blossom and bud, and fill the face of the world with fruit." (Isaiah 27:6)

Both Isaiah and Ezekiel (Ezekiel 36:8) prophesy about Israel's deserts blooming as though they are rejoicing, as the Hebrew people return from all over the world, where they have been scattered in exile.

From over 100 nations in the world, the Jewish people have been returning to the promised homeland Israel at a rate of over 2,000 people a month, as the first part of Isaiah 27:6a reads, "those who come He shall cause to take root in Jacob." The people are taking root, they are reclaiming the desert, building homes, schools, businesses and green houses. They are cultivating every crop you can imagine and planting every kind of tree for nuts, fruit and lumber.

Isaiah 27:6b reads, "Israel shall blossom and bud, and fill the face of the world with fruit." I was in Israel awhile back and I can testify that not only does the desert bloom in the Spring with the red lilies of the field Jesus spoke of in Matthew 6:28

and Luke 12:27, but Israel grows flowers all year-round in the desert now. Literally tens of millions of flowers of many varieties are grown and exported around the world.

Israel also grows and exports over 100 million pounds of fruits and vegetables a year. Up and down the Jordan River Valley and across Israel there are tens of thousands of greenhouses, producing enough to feed the population of Israel ten times over… God promised it… The Prophet's spoke it… We witness it... It's a Miracle!! How much more do you think we could do in His "shem" name? Isaiah 29:22-23 reads, "therefore thus says the Lord, who redeemed Abraham, concerning the house of Jacob: "Jacob shall not now be ashamed, nor shall his face now grow pale; but when he sees his children, the work of My hands, in his midst, they will hallow My "name" and hallow the Holy One of Jacob, and fear the God of Israel." Amen.

Those prophetic "Shemot" names are: Yeshua Messiah and Jesus Christ.

Philippians 2:9 reads, "Therefore God also has highly exalted Him and given Him the name which is above every name, that at the name of Jesus every knee should bow, of those in heaven and of those on the earth, and of those under the earth." ... Miracle.

Gospel Portion
Luke 5:12-39

Luke 5:12 records how a leper is cleansed…... Miracle.

Luke 5:16 tells of the paralytic who is healed…. Miracle.

Through the rest of Luke chapter 5, Yeshua Messiah makes it clear His mission is to call sinners unto repentance, reconciling us back to God... Miracle.

I've used the word "miracle" a lot in this Torah study, so let's define it. The Old Testament and the New Testament talk about signs, wonders and miracles. Jesus Himself said in Mark 16:15-18, "Go into all of the world and preach the gospel to every creature. He who believes and is baptized will be saved; but he who does not believe will be condemned. And these signs will follow those who believe: in My name they will cast out demons; they will speak with new tongues; they will take up serpents; and if they drink anything deadly, it will by no means hurt them; they will lay hands on the sick, and they will recover." Amen. Miracles!!!

We may define miracle as; A less common kind of God's interaction in the world where He arouses people's awe and wonder, and bears witness of Himself. This biblical definition for miracles points to the idea of God's power at work to arouse (awaken) people's wonder and amazement, bringing them to the only logical conclusion; God is real, God is here, God's overwhelming, awe-inspiring, never ending love for us is manifest in the great Name of His only begotten Son... Miracle.

Would you like to experience God's miracle of rebirth in your own life? Would you like to receive a new "shem" name? Let me explain the ABCs of God's miraculous salvation.

A. Admit, admit you have sinned and you are sorry you have.

B. Believe, believe Jesus died for that sin then rose from the grave on the third day.

C. Confess, confess with your mouth that Jesus is Lord and make Him King in your life.

Then read Romans 10:8-13, repenting and praying something like the words above. Make them your own heartfelt confession and pray, "Father, fill me with Your Spirit that I too can receive the miracle, that is salvation through Jesus Christ, in Jesus' Name I pray, Amen.

Bibliography for Shemot "names"
Interlinear Bible, The, Hendrickson publishing, 2006
New King James Version of the Bible, Thomas Nelson publishers, 2007
Strong's Complete Dictionary of the Bible Words, Thomas Nelson publishing, 1996

NOTES:

Va`era

"and I appeared"

Exodus 6:1-9:35
Ezekiel 28:25-29:21
Matthew 12:1-14

This Torah study titled "Va'era" in Hebrew means "and I appeared." It shows us that we need to recognize our God and His authority in our lives, we need to know that God wants a deeper more personal relationship with us. God wants us to know Him, not just about Him. He wants a relationship with us not just a religion about Him.

Additional Scripture

Psalm 8:4, 16:18   Matthew 10:32
Romans 1:21-25, 10:8-13

From GOD through Moses to YOU

This week's Torah Portion is in Exodus 6:1-9, 35 and is titled "Va'era" in Hebrew. It means "and I appeared."

Exodus 6:1 records that the Lord appeared to Moses.

Exodus 6:14 records the family lineage of Aaron and Moses.

Exodus 6:28 records Aaron being made Moses' spokesman.

Exodus 7:1 records the miracle of Aaron's rod.

Exodus 7:14 records the first plague: the waters turning to blood.

Exodus 8:1-30 records the second, third and fourth plagues: frogs, lice and flies.

Exodus 9:1-35 records the fifth, sixth and seventh plagues: livestock disease, boils and hail.

The Haftarah or Prophets' Portion is in Ezekiel 28:25-29:21

Ezekiel 28:25 records a future blessing for Israel.

Ezekiel 29:1-21 records a proclamation that Egypt will be plundered by Babylon.

The Gospel Portion is in Matthew 12:1-14

Matthew 12:1-14 records the controversy over Sabbath labor, Sabbath healing and the Pharisees' plan to kill Yeshua.

Va`era "and I appeared"

Torah Study
Exodus 6:1-9:35

Exodus 6:2-3 (Interlinear Bible) is where we get the title to this week's Torah Portion. Exodus 6:3 reads, "Va'era #7200," "and I appeared" to Abraham, to Isaac and to Jacob as God "Almighty #7706 El Shaddai," and by My Name "YHVH #3068 translated as Lord," I never made Myself known to them."

Here in the first part of Exodus 6, God is making Himself known as Yahweh, YHVH, instead of El Shaddai, God Almighty as the patriarchs Abraham, Isaac and Jacob knew Him. It's not like they never knew God, it's just that no one ever knew God in this intimate way before. The patriarchs knew a great deal about God and experienced His goodness in many ways, but they never had the revelation that was granted to Moses, Aaron and the people of this day. God wanted a deeper more personal relationship with them/us. Not only does God want people to know about Him, He desires for us to know Him personally, so we can establish a relationship with Him, rather than a religion about Him. Amen.

God began to reveal more and more about Himself through His many Names and attributes. This is understandable, because really if you think about it, how can God's greatness be contained or represented by just one name. I urge you to read the Scriptures with an open heart and an open mind, being willing to let God reveal Himself to you as your personal God.

Exodus 7:13 records, "and Pharaoh's heart grew hard, and he did not heed them, as the Lord had said." Pharaoh did not want to acknowledge any authority in his life except his own, and his selfish actions caused many lives to be lost. We should examine our own attitudes toward others with a soft heart, repenting in the Name of Jesus Christ.

God exalts Himself in many ways, His characteristics and attributes testify to His goodness. If all was said about Him, He would have to be spoken of by thousands of Names, but He is *one* God, *omnipotent* and *omnipresent; one* God.

The Egyptians, on the other hand, worshipped hundreds of idols but none of them were real. None could walk, none could talk, none could act, no, not one. Even Pharaoh himself, who was deemed a god incarnate on Earth, could not do or say anything that would alter even the smallest of YHVH's decrees in the land of Egypt or on Earth.

Exodus 7:13 (Interlinear Bible) reads, "and the heart of Pharaoh was hard, and he did not listen to them, as Jehovah had said." Here, the word "hardened" in Hebrew is "chazaq #2388, meaning to become arrogant, make stronger, to become prideful or to display strength, it can also mean to be caught or captured." God caught Pharaoh in his own words, his own actions and his sins, because of his pride.

Proverbs 16:18 reads, "Pride goes before destruction, and a haughty spirit before a fall." Amen. So, God hardens Pharaoh's heart to show Himself to be God *omnipotent*. There's *only one* God. Amen.

The Egyptians worshiped many hundreds of idols. They had

Va`era "and I appeared"

idols of fertility, idols of war, idols of rain, idols of thunder, idols of the underworld and heavens, sun and moon, idols for the river, lakes and streams, every species of wildlife was represented in their idol worship, male and female. With that in mind, let us look at the signs Moses and Aaron did before Pharaoh and his servants.

Aaron's miraculous rod, being turned into a snake, then devouring the snakes/rods of the Pharaoh's magicians. All the signs or plagues were designed of Yahweh, our Lord God, to show Himself as the one true and only God by directly attacking one of Egypt's main idol/gods.

The cobra, a symbol of Egypt's deadly power and authority, was part of Pharaoh's crown or headdress. As such, the first miracle was having Aaron's rod devour a snake created by Pharaoh's magicians. This was God's way of showing His authority and power over life and death.

The plague on the waters of Egypt was the first public plague. Water representing life, and the Nile River idol, a crocodile headed man figure, who was worshiped as a living, life bringing god, was turned to blood. In Leviticus 17:11 it records, "For the life of the flesh is in the blood, and I have given it to you upon the altar, to make atonement for your soul." The Nile River turning to blood, was God showing that He alone is the giver of life and it would be the blood of His Son that would bring eternal life to all the world.

The second plague: frogs. Every place and in everything, frogs appeared.

23

From GOD through Moses to YOU

The frog headed, human body idol represented fertility and was regarded as a symbol of renewal, life and happiness. This idol could now only be seen as a plague brought by God Almighty, Who multiplied their numbers into the millions, covering the land of Egypt with the stink of death; not the joy of birth.

The third and fourth plagues: lice and flies. When the lice came, Pharaoh's own magicians said: "This must be the finger of God!" (Exodus 8:19 Note: this verse is not recorded in the Interlinear Bible). The flies are associated with the idol of the underworld, death. By multiplying the flies, YHVH showed His power over the grave and death. And He did so again in John 20:21.

The fifth plague: livestock disease. The Egyptians worshiped idols shaped with the heads of bulls and horses on human bodies. Once again, God shows Himself to be greater than these idols. As all the livestock of the Egyptians fall dead, not a single animal of the Israelites was harmed.

The sixth plague: boils. Even Pharaoh himself was afflicted with boils, as well as the lice and the flies and the frogs. This was especially humiliating as the Pharaoh was considered to be the earthly representation of the sun-idol. He could do nothing, except to suffer along with his servants. God Almighty shows Himself superior yet again.

Hail was the seventh plague: wind, rain, thunder, lightning, all these storms were attributed to one deity or another, and our God, the God of the Hebrews, shows Himself the one in control of the very weather. This was so evident that Pharaoh admits that the Lord is righteous and asks Moses to stop the hail. Moses then informs the Pharaoh that the earth is the Lord's. But, after the hail had stopped, Pharaoh sinned yet again and hardened his heart (Exodus 9:27-35).

I want to ask you, just what would it take to convince you that God is real? What would it take to convince you that we need to recognize God and His authority in our lives? What would it take you to realize that God wants a relationship with us? Know this, God will shake us up first, if He has to; all so, He can say "Va'era," "and I appeared" to you.

I pray it doesn't take a plague to make you recognize Him and make Him sovereign ruler, God and friend in your life.

Haftarah Portion
Ezekiel 28:25-29:21

In Ezekiel 28:25-26, the Prophet describes God's blessings that will fall on future Israel and the Gentiles when they hallow Him, worship Him and adore Him; not just acknowledge Him religiously, but when they begin to know Him personally as their God.

Ezekiel 29:3 reads, "Speak, and say, 'Thus says the Lord God: "Behold, I am against you, O Pharaoh king of Egypt, O great monster that lies in the midst of his rivers, who has said, my river is my own; "I have made it for myself." Whoa! Now that's pride, a hard heart, represented by a half man half crocodile idol, worshiped by the ancient Egyptians then and even now as ancient cultural traditions are being re-embraced by this modern generation of New Age, neo-paganism and self-enlightenment seekers who are such a big part of the great apostasy of the end times (self being the key word).

Ezekiel 29:9 reads, "And the land of Egypt shall become desolate and waste; then they will know that I am the Lord, because he said, 'the river is mine, and I have made it.'" But the truth is, God Almighty created it all. He is El Shaddai, God as Creator, and He created the earth, the skies, the seas, rivers and the heavens. Then the Lord God Almighty created all their inhabitants. In ancient Egypt, we see the result of the creation, worshiping things created, rather than worshiping the Creator (Romans 1:21-25). The Creator is worthy to be praised and He desires a relationship with us. Think about it, the Creator wants to have fellowship with His creation! Honor and power be unto Him Who has said, "Va'era" and I appeared to Moses." That was then, and He will appear in your life now. Just look for Him, He's everywhere!

Gospel Portion
Matthew 12:1-14

Matthew 12:1-14 highlights the hardness of the Sadducees' and Pharisees' hearts. Because they didn't know God personally, they did not recognize Him when He walked among them. Sad, very sad. "Va'era" and appeared Jesus and said to them plainly in Matthew 11:25, "at that time Jesus answered and said, "I thank You, Father, Lord of heaven and earth, that You have hidden these things from the wise and prudent and have revealed them to babes."

Va`era "and I appeared"

And I appeared, "Va'era," doing signs and wonders all over ancient Egypt, for all the world to see; yet, they were still hard of heart. Over 1,000 years passed, and then God came to dwell among men as Yeshua Messiah, Jesus Christ, to do signs, wonders and miracles before man again, that we might develop a relationship with Him, again, as He had with Adam and Eve in the garden. It has been 2,000 years since God dwelt among men, and He still desires to have a relationship with us.

Psalm 8:4 reads, "What is man that You are mindful of him, and the son of man that You visit him?" Wow! Put yourself in that Scripture, I think it should read, "What am I, that You are mindful of me, and me the son of man that You visit me?" Think about the fact that the One and only Creator of all the heavens and Earth wants to have a personal relationship with you. Again Wow!

Well, there's only one way to that relationship and that's through Yeshua Messiah, Jesus and He is ever waiting for you. Do you want that relationship? Do you search for truth?

Has your hard heart started to soften? God wants to be able to appear to you personally. People, God is real and He wants a REAL-ationship with you and it's as easy to find as ABC.

A. Admit, admit you have sinned and you're sorry you did.
B. Believe, Jesus died for that sin, then rose from the grave on the third day.
C. Confess, confess with your mouth that Jesus is Lord and make Him King in your life.

From GOD through Moses to YOU

Read Romans 10:8-13 and Matthew 10:32, then pray with a repentant heart and ask the Father of us all to fill you with His Spirit that He would appear to you.

If you prayed that prayer in Jesus' Name, I would like to be the first one to welcome you to the family, second I would like to encourage you to tell a Messianic Rabbi, Pastor or Christian friend what you did, and third I would like to encourage you to contact us here at jewandgentileministiers.org

---

Bibliography for Va'era "and I appeared"
Interlinear Bible, The, Hendrickson publishing, 2016
New King James Version of the Bible, Thomas Nelson publishers, 2007
Strong's Complete Dictionary of Bible Words, Thomas Nelson publishers, 1996

NOTES:

Bo

"go in"

Exodus 10:1-13, 16
Jeremiah 46:13-28
Mark 3:6-19

This Torah study titled "Bo" in Hebrew means "go in." It teaches that God has chosen us to be His. Just as He chose the 12 tribes of Israel, and Jesus, Yeshua, chose His 12 disciples, we are chosen to be ensamples to the rest of the world.

Example is defined as: something chosen/selected to reflect or show the nature of or character of the original.

Ensample is defined as: something chosen/selected to be an exact duplicate, clone or copy of the original.

Additional Scripture

Mark 16:15-18   Malachi 3:11-12
1 Chronicles 28:9-10   1 Corinthians 3:16
Matthew 5:17-20, 6:34

From GOD through Moses to YOU

The Torah Portion this week is in Exodus 10:1-13:16 titled "Bo" in Hebrew meaning "go in".

Exodus 10:1 records the eighth plague: locusts.

Exodus 10:21 records the ninth plague: darkness.

Exodus 11:1 records the death of the firstborn is announced.

Exodus 12:1 records the initiation of the Passover.

Exodus 12:29 records the 10th plague: death of the firstborn.

Exodus 12:31 records the Exodus.

Exodus 12:43 record Passover regulations.

Exodus 13:1-16 records the firstborn being consecrated, the feast of unleavened bread, and the law of the firstborn.

The Haftarah or Prophets' Portion is in Jeremiah 46:13-28

Jeremiah 46:13-28 records Babylon will strike Egypt.

The Gospel Portion is in Mark 3:6-19

Mark 3:6-19 records the Pharisees' council to destroy Jesus and the selection of the 12 disciples.

Bo "go in"

Torah Study
Exodus 10:1-13, 16

The title for today's Torah study is found in Exodus 10:1 (Interlinear Bible), "and YHVH said to Moses, "Bo #935", "go in" to Pharaoh, for I have hardened his heart and the heart of his servants. So that I may set these signs of Mine in their midst."

God chose a man –Moses – to lead the children of Israel out of the land of Egypt, from under the hand of the oppressor – Pharaoh – to deliver them from death unto life – salvation – to set them apart in the wilderness – sanctification – to make them an ensample of Himself – justification – to show the world through them His might and majesty – glorification. Amen.

The eighth plague: locusts. Locusts as never seen before and never to be seen again. Yahweh, Lord God shows He is master over all creation saying, "behold, tomorrow I will bring locusts into your territory" (Exodus 10:4b). "I will bring locusts into your territory," against Egypt's idols of protection and provision. God exalts Himself, He, Yah is God that we should trust in Him only. Psalm 96:5 reads, "For all the gods of the peoples are idols, but the Lord made the heavens." Amen.

Jesus, Yeshua tells us, since we do not know what tomorrow will bring, we should trust fully in the Lord our God, who faithfully brings us another tomorrow (Matthew 6:34).

Malachi 3:11 reads, "And I will rebuke the devourer for your sakes, so that he will not destroy the fruits of your ground, nor shall the vine fail to bear fruit for you in the field," says the

From GOD through Moses to YOU

Lord of hosts; and all nations will call you blessed, for you will be a delightful land," says Yahweh Tsabaot #6635, the Lord of hosts." Know this, God is our protection and provision.

The ninth plague: darkness. Exodus 10:21 reads, "Then the Lord said to Moses, 'stretch out your hand toward heaven, that there may be darkness over the land of Egypt, darkness which may even be felt.'" My mind can hardly conceive that; it's even repulsed by the very idea. A darkness that can even be felt? Exodus 10:22 in the Interlinear Bible uses this expression, "vamash chosheck", "and (one may) feel darkness".

In that Scripture, the first word in Hebrew, "mashash #4959 is to feel or grope." The second Hebrew word, "chosheck #2822 is darkness, obscurity." These two Hebrew words together refer to "a darkness so thick you could feel it."

This manifestation of God's power would have severely affected the Egyptians. While they worshiped many idols, none were as revered as their sun idol. Even a solar eclipse would have made a startling impact on them, but an enshrouding darkness you could feel, that lasted three days was a full-on assault and defeat of the Egyptians' supposed gods and on their Pharaoh's supposed control over all nature. Pharaoh and all his servants, magicians, counselors and army were helpless before the true God of the heavens (Genesis 24:3, Eloah #433 HaShamayim #8064). The people must have been horrified. Yet, Pharaoh's heart was still hardened, producing deadly consequences.

Exodus 11 announces the 10th plague: the death of the firstborn. Chapter 12 is the initiation of the Passover. Again, God

Yahweh, shows Himself supreme as even the Pharaoh, the supposed sun god incarnate of Egypt holds his own dead son and cries out in anguish to his ineffectual, nonexistent deities and idols. Finally, Pharaoh would let the people go. Passover (Pesach #6453) was then established, commemorating God's deliverance of the Israelites from slavery and bondage to Egypt. But it also pointed to the coming deliverance and salvation of all the peoples of the earth, as it is but a shadow of the ultimate redemption that comes to us through the sacrifice of God's only begotten Son, our unspotted, unblemished, Lamb, Yeshua the Messiah, Jesus Christ. Luke 23:44-46, "Now it was about the sixth hour, and there was darkness over all the earth until the ninth hour. Then the sun was darkened, and the veil of the temple was torn in two. And when Jesus had cried out with a loud voice, He said, "Father, into your hands I commit My spirit." Having said this, He breathed His last." Amen.

We see by reading chapters 10 through 13 of Exodus, that God has chosen a people and appointed leaders over them. He wanted to separate them from the rest of the world, He desires for them to worship Him, and He also wants the rest of the world to know Him. He invites us to "Bo" go in to the Holy of Holies (as the veil has been torn) and meet Him there with praise and thanksgiving.

Haftarah Portion
Jeremiah 46:13-28

In Jeremiah 46:13-28, the Prophet tells us about a people, Israel. Chosen out of all the nations of the world; a people God would save in whole or in part, time and time again throughout the ages, solely for His purposes. Chosen that He may dwell among them and they would be a testimony and ensample to the rest of the world, showing His might and majesty in and through them. To Him be honor, glory, power and dominion forever (Matthew 6:13b).

In Jeremiah 46:17, the Prophet talks about the time of oppression the Israelites suffered in Egypt. Jeremiah 46:17 reads, "They cried there, Pharaoh king of Egypt, is but a noise, he has passed by the appointed time!" God made an example of Pharaoh for us in this generation to see what happens when we have such a hard heart toward Him. Like Egypt we worship and serve other gods, e.g., TV, sports, hobbies, or other worldly pursuits of the flesh take up so much of our time these days it's as if we worship them. The list of these activities is so extensive that I will not try to name them all. If you're wondering about something in your life, weigh it against this; if any pursuit in your life takes precedence over your relationship with God, meaning, if you spend more of your time doing those things than reading your Bible, going to church, fellowshipping with other Christians or praying, know this, it has become an idol in your life.

God invites us to "Bo #935 go in" to His presence. Psalm 100:2-3 reads, "Serve the Lord with gladness; "Bo" go in before His presence with singing, know that the Lord He is God; it is He Who has made us, and not we ourselves; we are His people and the sheep of His pasture. "Bo" go in to His gates with thanksgiving, and into His courts with praise. Be thankful to Him, and bless His Name." Amen.

Bo "go in"

Gospel Portion
Mark 3:6-9

In Mark 3:6-9 we see Jesus, Yeshua Messiah, call to Himself twelve men to disciple, teach, lead and make ensamples of. Yes, I said ensample as compared to examples.

Example is defined as: something selected/chosen to reflect or show the nature of or character of the original.

Ensample is defined as: something selected/chosen to be an exact duplicate of the original, copy of, or even clone.

Do you follow my train of thought here? It's like this, my Bible, your Bible, or even the book you're reading now, is an ensample. You can see it, touch it, read it, and understand it. Your Bible is a clone/ ensample of the original because not one jot or tittle has changed in the Torah since it was inspired of God and written by the hands of our forefathers (Matthew 5:17-20). An example is like a picture of the Bible, you can find a Bible with it, but you can't read it or understand it. Big difference.

God desires that we be ensamples of His Son, Yeshua, not examples. He has purposed that we should represent Him on this earth as His children, as Ambassadors of His Kingdom. Mark 16:15-18 reads, "Bo", "Go into all the world and preach the gospel to every creature. He who believes and is baptized will be saved; but he who does not believe will be condemned. And these signs will follow those who believe: in My name they will cast out demons; they will speak with new tongues; they will take up serpents; and if they drink anything deadly, it will by no means hurt them; they will lay hands on the sick, and they will recover."

God desires that we be ensamples of His Son. Look at your hands, hold them up, raise them up to the Lord, and make this profession of faith. "These hands will cast out demons! These hands will heal the sick! These hands will "bo" work for God! Amen, Amen, Amen!"

Moses led the twelve tribes of Israel out of Egypt into the promised land as an ensample of God's power. The people took the worship of Yahweh, the One True God, into the world basically as Evangelists. Compare the Old Testament to the New Testament, really, the way I think, compare the First Covenant and the Last Covenant.

1. Old Testament: even after seeing all the miracles done by God through Moses, Pharaoh's heart was still hard, and he plans to kill the Israelites by the Red Sea. (Exodus 14:5-9)

1. New Testament: even after seeing all the signs and miracles done by Jesus, the Sadducees and Pharisees plan to kill Him. (Matthew 26:1-4)

2. Old Testament: God chooses Israel and Moses leads the twelve tribes of Israel out into the wilderness, finally to Canaan to bring the worship of the *one true* God into the promised land. (Exodus 3:4-8)

2. New Testament: Jesus chooses twelve men to be disciples and sends them forth to preach the Gospel to the whole world (Matthew 28:16-20).

Bo "go in"

Old Testament and New Testament together are the fulfillment of prophecy and promise. I want you to know, God of all creation has chosen you, to bring you out of the world, to make you a showpiece of His glory for all the world to see. God has chosen you, what will it take for you to choose him? Famine, pestilence, sword, a darkness that you can feel? Don't be like Pharaoh or the Pharisee, hard of heart and prideful. Instead, be like the disciples, who were willing to be led. Amen. "Bo" go into all the world, your world; your family, your neighborhood, your town, and your work. Anyplace you go is your mission field.

People, beloved of God, realize this; God has already chosen you! Read this next Scripture from 1 Chronicles 28:9-10 NKJV with the understanding that you, your body and mind are to be the dwelling place for God's Holy Spirit. Insert your name where it says Solomon (Shlomo), then make this prayer of David your own.

"As for you, Shlomo (your name) my son/daughter, know the God of your father. Serve Him wholeheartedly and with desire in your being; for Adonai searches all hearts and understands all the inclinations of people's thoughts. If you seek Him, He will let Himself be found by you; but if you abandon Him, He will reject you forever. See now that Adonai has chosen you to build a house for the sanctuary; so be strong and do it!" (1 Chronicles 28:9)

God has already chosen you. You are to be that Tabernacle/Temple, so that God's Holy Spirit can dwell inside you (1 Corinthians 3:16).

From GOD through Moses to YOU

God has already chosen you, and He desires that you choose Him. If you want to choose Him now "Bo" go pray, it's easy as ABC.

A. Admit, at that you have sinned and repent of them.
B. Believe, believe that Jesus died for those sins and rose from the grave on the third day.
C. Confess, confess with your mouth that Jesus is Lord and make Him King in your life.

Read Romans 10:8-13 and Mark 16:16, then pray a prayer of repentance and pray that the Father will fill you with His Spirit, so you can begin to live your life according to His will.

If you prayed that prayer, first I would like to welcome you to the family, second, I encourage you to talk with a Messianic Rabbi, Pastor or a Christian friend. They will know what to do next.

If you prayed that prayer, I would like to know and celebrate your new life. Contact us here at jewandgentileministries.org

---

Bibliography for Bo "go in"
Interlinear Bible, The, Hendrickson publishing, 2006
New King James Version of the Bible, Thomas Nelson publishers, 2007
Strong's Complete Dictionary of Bible Words, Thomas Nelson publishing, 1996

Beshalach

"when sent"

Exodus 13:17-17:16
Judges 4:4-5:31
Matthew 5:1-48

This Torah study titled "Beshalach" in Hebrew means "when sent." It teaches that God delivers us out of the hand of the oppressor. Whether we are oppressed physically, mentally or spiritually, God is our deliverer and our blessed hope of an eternal future in the promised land.

Additional Scripture

Hebrews 13:15   Matthew 11:28-29
Psalm 108:12-13   John 3:16
Romans 10:8-13

From GOD through Moses to YOU

This week's Torah Portion is titled "Beshalach #7971" in Hebrew meaning "when sent." It is found in Exodus 13:17-17:8.

Exodus 13:17 records the beginning of Israel's wilderness journeys.

Exodus 14:1 records the Red Sea crossing.

Exodus 15:1 records the song of Moses.

Exodus 15:20 records the song of Miriam.

Exodus 16:1 records God giving manna from heaven.

Exodus 17:1 records water gushing from the rock.

Exodus 17:8 records Israel's victory over the Amalekites.

The Haftarah or Prophets' Portion is in Judges 4:4-5:31

Judges 4:4 records that Deborah, a Prophetess, was judging Israel.

Judges 5:1 records the song of Deborah.

The Gospel Portion is in Matthew 5:1-48

Matthew 5:1 records the Beatitudes.

Matthew 5:13 records the Similitudes. Salt, light, Jesus fulfills the law, murder, adultery, divorce, oaths, retaliation and love.

Torah Study
Exodus 13:17-17:16

Throughout our Torah readings in Exodus we see our God, Yahweh, deliver the children of Israel out of the hands of their oppressors. God delivers Israel out from under the oppression of Pharaoh and the polytheistic culture they were surrounded by and really, after 430 years, many Israelites were a part of. In Exodus, chapters 13-17 God delivers Israel from Pharaoh's physical oppression of bondage and hard labor as well as the spiritual oppression of offering sacrifices to hundreds of false gods that demanded the Israelites engage in immoral, even perverted rites and rituals. God delivered them by sending someone (Moses) as a type of Redeemer to bring them out from under physical, mental and spiritual oppression (a type of deliverance). He led them to the Red Sea (Ha Yam #3220 The sea) where He parts the waters that they may pass through them (a type of baptism). When Pharaoh tries to follow, the Red Sea, closes on Pharaoh and his army, killing them (the effect of baptism purging, washing us from the past and sin). Moses then takes Israel into the wilderness (a form of sanctification) setting them apart for instruction (spiritual education). Whereby they might be deemed worthy, not by their own works but by the hand of the Redeemer Moses/Jesus (that's justification). Receiving the reward of the promised land, an eternal inheritance in Christ Jesus (that's glorification).

We see this pattern over and over again throughout the Bible, Old Testament and New. Oppression, Redemption, Deliverance, Salvation, Baptism, Sanctification, Education, Justification and Glorification! Hallelujah, Amen. Sing praises to God for our deliverance, Moses did "Beshalach" when sent to the wilderness.

"The Lord is my strength and my song and He has become my salvation; He is my God, and I will praise Him; my father's God, and I will exalt Him." (Exodus 15:2)

Haftarah Portion
Judges 4:4-5:31

We see the process of Oppression, Redemption, Deliverance, Salvation, Baptism, Sanctification, Education, Justification and Glorification again in Judges 4:4-5:31, as Israel is being oppressed by Jabin, king of Canaan. Then Israel is saved, this time being delivered by the hand of Deborah, a Prophetess [yay girls!] Don't think this is the only recorded time where Israel was delivered by a woman. The book of Esther comes to mind, also, the commander of the Canaanite Army, Sisera, was killed by Jael, Heber's wife. Anyway, we see the process of Oppression, Redemption, deliverance, Salvation, Baptism, Sanctification, Education, Justification and Glorification repeat itself over and over throughout the Old Testament, most notably in the stories of Noah and Moses, but just read through the Prophets and you'll see it time and again.

These readings from the Torah and Haftarah (Exodus and Judges) both include songs of praise and thanksgiving for victory.

The song of Moses in Exodus 15 is a song of praise the children of Israel sang the day they were delivered from Pharaoh's oppressive hand. In verse two of the song of Moses (Exodus 15:2), they use a unique word for praise, not the usual "hallelujah" that we are used to hearing, but another Hebrew word "tehillah # 8416 meaning song of praise," which conveys the meaning "to bring God beauty by the sacrifice of our lips."

Hebrews 13:15 reads, "Therefore by Him let us continually offer the sacrifice of praise to God, that is the fruit of our lips, giving thanks to His name." Wow!! Think on this, "Beshalach," "when sent" out to battle and you are having a bad day. When you are "being oppressed by this world," try singing praises to God, for Heaven will take notice and begin to change your circumstances. Psalm (tehillah #8416) 108:12-13 reads, "Give us help from trouble, for the help of man is useless. Through God we will do valiantly, for it is He who shall tread down our enemies." Amen.

The reading from our Haftarah Portion in Judges 4:4-5:31 ends with the song of Deborah (Judges 5:1-31), and in the third verse of the song, the Hebrew word for praise is also different from the usual "hallelujah #1984." It is the word "zamar #2167 to make music in praise of God," which conveys the meaning "to celebrate by playing instruments and giving voice, singing forth songs of praise to the Lord."

1. Only He is worthy of praise, hallelujah!
2. Only He is worthy of worship, tehillah!
3. Only He is worthy of our adoration, zamar!

Gospel Portion
Matthew 5:1-48

All of chapter 5 in Matthew deals with the Beatitudes and Similitudes which we know as the sermons on the mount.

From GOD through Moses to YOU

These teachings are what Jesus, Yeshua, preached "Beshalach" when sent to start His earthly ministry in the area around the Sea of Galilee. Most theologians agree these series of discourses are the greatest sermons ever preached, Amen.

In Matthew chapter 5 are Jesus' Words written in red in my Bible. Like words that are penned with His precious blood. The Beatitudes and the Similitudes offer instruction, edification and clarification of the Mosaic commandments and Torah set down by the forefathers. No, the 10 Commandments are not dead. Yeshua clarified the Torah, telling us we are not to try and uphold the letter of the law, but to transcend the law in the attitude of our hearts.

Problem? Yes, because even the scribes and Pharisees could not uphold the whole Torah, so what are we as mere people to do? Problem yes? Well, problem no, see, God foresaw all of this and sent His Son, Jesus, to fulfill all the requirements of the law for us (Matthew 5:17-20). Only a perfect man could satisfy the righteous standards God had set.

"Yeshua Hamashiach #4886 the anointed One," came as our "Redeemer #1350 gaal," our "Savior #3467 yasha," too free us from the oppression of this world. Yes, we are to live our lives as law-abiding, upstanding, moral citizens, but only Jesus could fulfill God's righteous standards. He is our Salvation and Deliverance from oppression. He is our Baptism, the washing and cleansing from sin. He is our Sanctification, Education and Instruction in the wilderness and He is our blessed hope, our Justification unto our eternal reward our Glorification!!! Hallelujah! Tehillah! Zamar!

Beshalach "when sent"

If you want to be set free from the oppressions of this world, in whatever form they have taken in your life, alcohol, drugs, lust, greed, hate, pride, sloth or unforgiveness, I want you to know you can call out to Jesus and He will help you. Matthew 11:28-29 reads, "Come to Me, all you who labor and are heavy laden, and I will give you rest. Take My yoke upon you and learn from Me, for I am gentle and lowly in heart, and you will find rest for your souls, for My yoke is easy and My burden is light." Amen.

People, beloved of God, if you want to end oppression in your life, you can begin by applying the ABCs of freedom in your life.

A. Admit, admit you have sinned and repent for those sins.
B. Believe, believe Jesus died for those sins, then rose from the grave on the third day.
C. Confess, confess with your mouth that Jesus is Lord and make Him King in your life.

Read Romans 10:8-13 and John 3:16. Pray a prayer of repentance for the wrongs you have done in your life and ask the Father to fill you with His Spirit that you may be set free of all that oppresses you. Pray in Jesus' Name, thanking the Lord, Amen.

If you prayed that prayer go tell a Pastor, Messianic Rabbi or Christian friend they will know what to do next.

Bibliography for Beshalach "when sent"
Interlinear Bible, The, Hendrickson publishing, 2006
New King James Version of the Bible, Thomas Nelson publishers, 2007
Strong's Complete Dictionary of Bible Words, Thomas Nelson publishing, 1996

From GOD through Moses to YOU

NOTES:

Yitro

"excellence"

Exodus 18:1-20:23
Isaiah 6:1-7:6, 9:5-7
Matthew 6:1-8

This Torah study titled "Yitro" in Hebrew means "excellence." Yitro, Moses's father-in-law, gives Moses advice on how to judge the people. Moses was to choose able men who fear God, men of truth, who hate covetousness, then teach them the statutes and law. He would then set them over the tribes so they could judge every small matter, freeing Moses to judge the great matters and bring the difficult cases before God. This Torah study teaches that if we were to live by the laws God has established we would not need to be ruled by man.

Additional Scripture

Genesis 1:26, 6:6-8   Psalm 119:33-34
Exodus 12:37   Romans 10:8-13
Isaiah 7:14, 9:6-7   Matthew 5:1-31, 11:28, 22:36-40

From GOD through Moses to YOU

This week's Torah Portion is in Exodus 18:1-20:23 and is titled "Yitro #3503" which means in Hebrew "preeminence or excellence"

Exodus 18 records Yitro's advice.

Exodus 19 records God introducing Himself to the Israelites.

Exodus 2:1-17 records the 10 Commandments.

Exodus 20:18-21 records the people fearing God's presence.

Exodus 20:22-26 records the law of the altar.

The Haftarah or Prophets' Portion is in Isaiah 6:1-7, 9:5-7

Isaiah 6 records Isaiah's call to be a Prophet.

Isaiah 9:5-7 records a prophecy concerning Yeshua.

The Gospel Portion is in Matthew 6:1-8:1

Matthew 6 records the Similitudes about charitable deeds, prayer, fasting and wealth.

Matthew 7 records the Similitudes about judging, asking, the golden rule, wide and narrow gates, false and true teaching, the true way into the Kingdom, the parable of two builders, and the people's response to His sermons.

Matthew 8:1 records that great multitudes followed Him.

Yitro "excellence"

Torah Portion
Exodus 18:1-20:23

Exodus 18:1 (Interlinear Bible) is where we get our title "Yitro #3503" for the Torah study this week. Exodus 18:1 reads, "and Jethro "Yitro" the priest of Midian, the father-in-law of Moses, heard all which God had done for Moses, and for His people Israel, that Jehovah had caused Israel to go out from Egypt."

Jethro, "Yitro #3503" is from the Hebrew root word "yathar #3498" and means "preeminence or excellence." Another related word "yithrah #3502" means "abundance and riches." So, Moses' father-in-law was not only a respected and wealthy man, he was also wise. Jethro saw immediately the great need for governance in and for the new nation of Israel. He knew that it would be impossible for one man to try and judge all the nation's problems and disputes. His advice to Moses was to select men of good standing, able men, men of truth, hating covetousness. Then place such men over the tribes to be rulers of thousands, rulers of hundreds, rulers of fifties, and rulers of tens and let them judge the people of the new nation of Israel at all times. This way, Moses would only have to judge the great matters and bring them before God.

In Genesis 1:26 God says, "Let Us make man in Our image, according to Our likeness; let them have dominion over the fish of the sea, over the birds of the air, and over the cattle, over all the earth and over every creeping thing that creeps on the earth."

Did you catch that? Man was created to have governance, to reign, to rule, to have dominion over all the earth from the very beginning, but there's something else here that most of us miss because, it's not written in black and white. Really, it's what's not written, and that was for man to have dominion or rule over another man. Did you catch that? Man was never intended to have rule, governance or dominion over another man. God never intended for men to rule over one another We were intended to be in fellowship with God, to live in love, peace and in harmony in paradise, Heaven on Earth, the Garden of Eden He created for us, the Kingdom of Heaven on Earth.

Then, man fell. Adam sinned, he rebelled, he ate of the fruit from the tree of the knowledge of good and evil. He chose of his own free will to disobey God's rule, thereby ceding man's dominion to Satan. Anyway, that's a whole other sermon, so, God let man, by his free will try to run things under the influence of Satan and naturally only chaos ruled until God said no more. Genesis 6:6-8 says, "and the Lord was sorry that He had made man on the earth, and He was grieved in His heart. So the Lord said, "I will destroy man whom I have created from the face of the earth, both man and beast, creeping thing and birds of the air, for I am sorry that I have made them." But Noah found grace in the eyes of the Lord."

So, God started over with Noah, and for another couple of thousand years He let man try again to run things himself. Still the earth was not right, so He chose a people from among the nations to make His, to set apart, to sanctify. He brought them out into the wilderness and there at Mount Sinai, He introduced Himself to them. Exodus 19:17 reads, "and Moses brought the people out of the camp to meet with God and they stood at the foot of the mountain."

God introduced Himself to around two million-plus people that day!

Exodus 12:37 records about 600,000 men besides women and children came out of Egypt and verse 38 records a mixed multitude went out with them also. This group consisted of other ethnic groups that had their own reasons for leaving Egypt. They were conquered peoples, prisoners of war made to be slaves just like Israel. There were Libyans from Libya, Cushites from Ethiopia, people from all over most of Africa and the Middle East. Think about it, Egypt is defeated by God and their military was drowned in the Red Sea. There was nothing preventing all of these slaves from going home. There had to have been an Exodus to the West and South as big or bigger than the Exodus of the Israelites to the East.

At Mount Sinai, God introduced Himself to the multitudes in the third month. That day He restarted the covenant He had with their forefathers and outlined the laws that were to govern their lives, the 10 Commandments. But the people were afraid of God's presence and asked that Moses speak to them instead; once again putting a man to rule over them and not the sovereign Lord, King of all Heaven and Earth (Eloheynu Melech Ha Olam).

Haftarah Portion
Isaiah 6:1-7, 9:5-7

Isaiah 6:1 shows God's proper place in our lives, now spiritually and in our future physically. The Throne where the Lord is seated, high and exalted, represents His eternal sovereign and universal rule, He is high above all other kings, He is "Yitro" excellence, but at the same time He is concerned for the welfare of His people. So, in Isaiah 7:14 it says, "Therefore the Lord Himself will give you a sign: Behold, the virgin shall conceive and bear a Son, and shall call His name "Immanuel #6005 God with us." Isaiah 9:6 – 7, tells us the government will be on His shoulder, and His name will be called Wonderful, Counselor, Mighty God, Everlasting Father, Prince of Peace and of the increase of His government and peace there will be no end."

God's laws will be established in the earth again because He is "Yitro" excellence. God's laws, not man's laws. God gave the 10 Commandments, not man. I can't stress this point enough in light of the apostate attitudes that have been adopted by so many people in this country. In recent years those lost and misguided individuals demanded plaques, statues and monuments bearing the 10 Commandments in and around "government" buildings and schools be taken down, put out of sight, out of the public view. We know that history repeats itself, and just like at Mount Sinai, the people today do not want to hear the Voice of the Sovereign Lord. Amen.

Gospel Portion
Matthew 6:1-8:1

Matthew chapters 5-7 are all written in red in my Bible, recording what Jesus spoke. In this passage, Jesus, Yeshua, clarifies the 10 Commandments. He explains that it's not just the letter of the law we are to hold onto, but we are to aspire to an attitude of the heart, going above and beyond the 10 Commandments. Maybe we can and maybe we can't, as it is recorded that only Yeshua fulfilled all the requirements of the law. He did it for us, so we should be happy to at least fulfill the 10 Commandments as our personal service to Him.

Jesus, Yeshua having fulfilled the laws of Moses and the Prophets (the whole Torah), simplifies them for us. John 13:34 reads, and again this is written in red, "A new commandment I give you, that you love one another; as I have loved you, that you also love one another." And in Matthew 22:36-40, Jesus is asked which is the greatest commandment in the law and He replies, "you shall love the Lord your God with all your heart, with all your soul, and with all your mind." This is the first and the great commandment. And the second is like it; "you shall love your neighbor as yourself." On these two commandments hang all the law and the prophets."

Jesus, Yeshua, our unspotted, unblemished, sacrificial Lamb became our "Yitro" excellence, that we might become excellence through Him. This Torah study teaches that if we would live by the laws God established, we would not need to be ruled by any other man.

People, beloved of God, we will never be completely free of the oppressive law and governance of man in this world, but we do have the promise of a better, more perfect and just future if we accept Jesus as Lord of our lives now. Matthew 11:28 reads, "Come to Me, all you who labor and are heavy laden, and I will give you rest. Take My yoke "Torah" upon you and learn from

From GOD through Moses to YOU

Me, for I am gentle and lowly in heart, and you will find rest for your souls. For My yoke "Torah" is easy and My burden is light." People, we do need to fear God's Voice!

Psalm 119:33-34 says, "Teach me, O Lord, the way of Your statutes, and I shall keep it to the end. Give me understanding and I shall keep Your law; indeed, I shall observe it with my whole heart."

If you want to be set free from the law of sin and death and embrace the law of love and life eternal, it's as easy as ABC.

A. Admit, admit you have sinned and you are sorry you did.
B. Believe, believe Jesus died for that sin, then rose from the grave on the third day.
C. Confess, confess with your mouth that Jesus is Lord and make Him King in your life.

Read Romans 10:8-13 and John 3:16, then pray a prayer of repentance and ask God the Father to fill you with His Spirit so you too can live by His law and no longer by your own law, thus becoming "Yitro" excellence in His sight.

If you prayed that prayer go tell a Pastor, Messianic Rabbi, or a Christian friend. They will know what to do next.

Bibliography for Yitro "excellence"
Interlinear Bible, The, Hendrickson publishing, 2006
New King James Version of the Bible, Thomas Nelson publishers, 2007
Strong's Complete Dictionary of Bible Words, Thomas Nelson publishing, 1996

Mishpatim

"judgments"

Exodus 21:1-24:18
Jeremiah 34:8-22, 33:25-26
Luke 7:1-8:3

This Torah study titled "Mishpatim" in Hebrew means "judgments." We may not understand God's judgments but, they are all just and righteous. One of the many Hebrew titles for God is "Shophat," which means judge. Justice is ultimately rooted, not in a collection of laws or rules, but in the very character and nature of God. As judge of the whole earth, God is the only One competent to measure the contents and motivations of our hearts.

Additional Scripture

Psalm 119:137
John 5:22-24
1 Corinthians 11:3
2 Corinthians 5:10
Matthew 25:31-46

Revelation 20:11-15
Jeremiah 31:33
John 3:16-18
Leviticus 26:14-17

From GOD through Moses to YOU

This Torah Portion titled "Mishpatim" in Hebrew means "judgments #4941." It is found in Exodus 21:1-24:18

Exodus 21:31-46 records laws concerning servants, violence and animal control.

Exodus 22 records personal responsibility for property.

Exodus 23:1-33 records that there will be justice for all, the law of the Sabbath, the Spring feasts are instituted and the Lord sends an Angel before Israel.

Exodus 24:1-18 records Israel agreeing to the covenant, then Moses goes up onto the mountain with 70 elders.

The Haftarah or Prophets' Portion is in Jeremiah 34:8-22 and 33:25-26

Jeremiah 34:8 records the penalty for treacherous treatment of slaves.

Jeremiah 33:25-26 the Lord warns Israel to obey.

The Gospel Portion is in Luke 7:1-8:3

Luke 7:1-49 records the centurions' servant being healed, a widow's son is raised from the dead, John the Baptist's questions are answered, Yeshua praises John, Yeshua criticizes His generation, a woman anoints Jesus's feet and the parable of the two debtors.

Luke 8:1-3 records many who provide substance for Yeshua.

Mishpatim "judgments"

Torah Portion
Exodus 21:1-24:18

Exodus 21:1 (Interlinear Bible) reads, "and these are the "Mishpatim #4941" judgments which you shall put before them." This is where we get the title for our portion this week.

The Hebrew word translated as "judgments," "Mishpatim" is used extensively (118 times) as "justice." Mishpatim is also used as "ordinances" a total of 79 times and is used for the words: sentence, procedure, charge, claim, and customs. So, we can see this word is used to help establish rules, regulations and ordinances necessary for the government of the fledgling nation Israel, these "Mishpatim" judgments differ from God's law, i.e., the 10 Commandments, as opposed to man's laws, i.e., apodictic laws, (those being made of necessity for governance). Exodus 21-23 are just the beginning of the Mishpatim "judgments" that Moses and the appointed men "shophat" establish for the people of Israel.

One of the many titles for God is "Shaphat #8199." In Hebrew it means "judge" and is a very appropriate title for our God, as He is "judge of all the earth (Genesis 18:25)." Justice is ultimately rooted, not in a collection of law or rules, but in the very character and nature of God. As judge of the whole earth, He "God" is the only one competent to measure or judge the motivations of our hearts. Amen.

Psalm 119:137 reads, "Righteous are You, O Lord, and upright are Your judgments."

The Psalmist, King David must have loved the Mishpatim and studying Torah because he used the phrase, "teach me Your statutes or teach me Your ways" over and over again.

Haftarah Portion
Jeremiah 33:25-26, 34:8-22

In Jeremiah 34:8-22, we see the typical "Mishpatim" judgments of the Old Testament. When Israel did good, blessings from Heaven abounded; in like manner, when Israel does bad, God punishes them. Judge and judgments are not words we as modern Christians warm to, particularly those who have grown up with a distorted image of God as a wrathful, judgmental old-timer frowning down on us, waiting to punish us as soon as we break a rule. (not so!)

Yes, God does judge and punish sin, whether in this life or the next, but there is justice in the judgment. Deuteronomy 32:3-4 reads, "For I proclaim the name of the Lord: ascribe greatness to our God He is the Rock #6697 tsur, His work is perfect; for all His ways are justice, a God of truth and without injustice; Righteous and upright is He." Amen.

"This is the word that came to Jeremiah from the Lord, after King Zedekiah had made a covenant with all the people who were at Jerusalem to proclaim liberty to them: that every man should set free his male and female slaves – a Hebrew man or woman – that no one should keep a Jewish brother in bondage. Now when all the princes and all the people, who had entered into the covenant, heard that everyone should set free his male and female slaves, that no one should keep them in bondage anymore, they obeyed and let them go. But afterward, they changed their minds and made the male and female slaves return, whom they had set free, and brought them into subjection as male and female slaves." (Jeremiah 34:8-11)

When Israel sinned and broke covenant this time, it was because they enslaved those whom they had previously freed. The people knew that they broke the law; the covenant.

The king issued a decree to set the slaves free. Mandates, decrees and commands, the proclamations made by a sovereign king were being broken and ignored, a violation that was punishable by death. Well, it's even more serious than that. God has said in Jeremiah 31:33, "This is the covenant that I will make with the house of Israel after those days, says the Lord: "I will put My law in their minds, and write it on their hearts; and I will be their God, and they shall be My people."

So, you see they, we, really have no excuse because God put this thing in us that we call a conscience, but many choose not to listen to it. Some may pretend not to know the written law but really, deep down inside we know what is right.

We are encouraged in 2 Timothy 2:15 to "Study to show yourself approved to God, a workman that needs not to be ashamed, rightly dividing the word of truth."

People, rightly divide the Word of truth. Read your Bibles for yourselves! Do not be misled by "single judgment" or "general judgment" theories that are the invention of the early Catholic Church and not taught in the Word of God.

From GOD through Moses to YOU

There are at least five separate "Mishpatim" judgments found in the Bible, and they differ as to when, where and why. What they do have in common is the "Shaphat" judge is the one and the same in every case, and that is Jesus Christ, Yeshua Messiah (John 5:22).

Everyone who has ever lived, and every nation that has ever existed will one day stand in judgment before our Lord Jesus.

The five judgments referred to are:

1. The judgment of the believer's sins (John 5:24).
2. The judgment of the believer's self (1 Corinthians 11:3).
3. The judgment of the believer's works (2 Corinthians 5:10).
4. The judgment of the nations (Matthew 25:31-46).
5. The judgment of the wicked (Revelation 20:11-15).

I encourage all my readers to focus on number two, the judgment of the believer's self. Because if we can rightly judge ourselves in this life, we can look forward to God's perfect and righteous judgment in the next life.

Gospel Portion
Luke 7:1-8:3

We see in the Gospels that Jesus didn't spend a lot of time judging sin, He condemned some actions and attitudes, but He didn't judge a person's sin, rather He forgave their sin. Jesus was already putting into action God's plan of redemption for the world. He knew sin would be judged on the cross (John 5:24). He would take the world's sins upon Himself, suffer and

Mishpatim "judgments"

die for them. Because under Old Testament law, sin needed a sacrifice for forgiveness, Yeshua became that sacrifice for us. He was judged guilty for us and was put to death for us. He shed His blood for us on Calvary to atone that sin for us. That's love, awesome love.

"And as Moses lifted up the serpent in the wilderness, even so must the Son of Man be lifted up, that whoever believes in Him should not perish but have eternal life. For God so loved the world that He gave His only begotten Son, that whoever believes in Him should not perish but have everlasting life. For God did not send His Son into the world to condemn the world, but that the world through Him might be saved. He who believes in Him is not condemned; but he who does not believe is condemned already, because he has not believed the name of the only begotten Son of God." (John 3:14-18)

People, beloved of God, there has already been a "Mishpatim" judgment on your sins. Your sins have already been judged. Psalm 103:12 says, "As far as the east is from the west, so far has He removed our transgressions from us."

All you have to do is accept forgiveness and repent, it's as easy as ABC.

A. Admit, admit you have sinned and ask forgiveness for those sins.
B. Believe, believe Jesus died for those sins, then rose from the grave on the third day.
C. Confess, confess with your mouth that Jesus is Lord and make Him King in your life.

From GOD through Moses to YOU

Read Romans 10:8-13, then pray a prayer of repentance and ask Father God to fill you with His Spirit so you can judge yourself here and now. Pray in Jesus' Name Amen.

If you prayed that prayer, first, I would like to welcome you to the family of God. Second, I would encourage you to tell a Pastor, Messianic Rabbi or a Christian friend what you just did. They will know what to do next. Or contact us here at jewandgentileministries.org

---

Bibliography for Mishpatim "judgments"
Interlinear Bible, The Hendrickson publishing, 2006
New King James Version of the Bible, Thomas Nelson publishers, 2007
Strong's Complete Dictionary of the Bible Words, Thomas Nelson publishing, 1996

NOTES:

Terumah

"offerings"

Exodus 25:1-27:19
1 Kings 5:12-6:13
Matthew 12:46-13:58

This Torah study titled "Terumah" in Hebrew means "offering;" a heave offering, a contribution offered by lifting up, something offered willingly. The heave offering was taken from the best of all the other offerings and set apart for Yahweh. It was assigned to the Priest's family for use as food for all the family members, male and female, provided they were ceremonially clean. Yeshua presented Himself, willingly, to be lifted up as the best of all sacrifices to God for all who would ask forgiveness of sin and repent (1 Corinthians 15:20). "Terumah" the firstfruits of a crop which anticipates and guarantees the ultimate offering of the whole crop (James 1:8). We are that crop.

Additional Scripture

John 8:12	James 1:18
John 6:48	1 Corinthians 15:20
John 12:32-33	Matthew 3:11

From GOD through Moses to YOU

This Torah Portion is titled "Terumah 8641" in Hebrew and means "offerings," contributions given willingly to be lifted up and waved before the Lord. It is found in Exodus 25:1-27:19.

Exodus 25:1-9 records free will offerings collected to build the sanctuary.

Exodus 25:10-22 records plans to build the Ark of the Testimony.

Exodus 25:23-30 records plans to build the table for the Showbread.

Exodus 25:31-40 records plans to build the gold Menorah.

Exodus 26 records plans to build the Tabernacle.

Exodus 27:1-8 records plans for the Altar of Burnt Offering.

Exodus 27:9-19 records plans for the Court of the Tabernacle.

The Haftarah or Prophets' Portion is in 1 Kings 5:12-6;13

1 Kings 5:12-18 records that the Lord gave Solomon wisdom.

1 Kings 6:1-13 records Solomon building the Temple.

The Gospel Portion is in Matthew 12:46-13:58

Matthew 12:46 records how Jesus describes true brethren.

Matthew 13:1-58 records the parables of the soil, of wheat and tares, the mustard seed, leaven, tares explained, hidden treasure, the householder and Jesus' rejection at Nazareth.

Terumah "offerings"

Torah Portion
Exodus 25:1-27:19

Exodus 25:1-3 (Interlinear Bible) reads, "and Jehovah spoke to Moses, saying speak to the sons of Israel, and let them take an "offering #8641 Terumah" for Me from every man whose heart impels him – let them take My "Terumah" and this is the "Terumah" which you shall take from them: gold, and silver, and bronze."

The type of offering here is mentioned three times, three being the numeric equivalent of the Hebrew letter "gimel," the first letter in the Hebrew word "gadol" which means great, gigantic and enormous. Three also represents the plurality of Elohim, Father, Son, Holy Spirit; so, "Terumah" offerings would be enormous free will offerings, lifted up and presented to our awesome God! Hallelujah! Free will offering being key here. Exodus 25:2 puts it this way, "Speak to the children of Israel, that they bring Me an offering. From everyone who gives it willingly with his heart you shall take My offering."

God commands that we sacrifice, serve and obey Him, but, and it is important that you hear this, God does not need these gifts. The only gifts with any value are the ones you give willingly, freely, and gladly. Amen.

God wanted Moses to collect these gifts, so they, Moses and the children of Israel, could build a Tabernacle, a sanctuary where the Lord could dwell among them.

The offering, being lifted up, the heave offering, was that portion of all offerings, the best of the best that was levied, taken up and set apart for Yahweh. Heave, lift up, a wave offering before the Lord. The best of the wave offerings, the firstfruits of the oil, wine and grain.

These offerings were then assigned to the Priest's families for use as food by all the members male and female, provided they were ceremonially clean. Yeshua presented Himself willingly, to be lifted up as the best of all sacrifices. John 12:32-33 reads, "And I, if I am lifted up from the earth, will draw all peoples to Myself." This He said, signifying by what death He would die." The firstfruits of a crop, lifted up, raised, which anticipates and guarantees the ultimate offering of the whole crop.

"But now Christ is risen from the dead, and has become the firstfruits of those who have fallen asleep. For since by a man death came, by Man also came the resurrection of the dead. For as in Adam all die, even so in Christ all shall be made alive. But each one in his own order: Christ the firstfruits, afterwards those who are Christ's at His coming" (1 Corinthians 15:20-23). Amen, we are that crop!

"Every good gift and every perfect gift is from above, and comes down from the Father of lights, with whom there is no variation or shadow of turning. Of His own will He brought us forth by the word of truth, that we might be a kind of firstfruits of His creatures" (James 1:17-18). Amen.

In Exodus 25-27, we see the preparations for the Tabernacle of God, the building of the Ark of the Covenant, building the table for the Showbread, making the Gold Menorah and the Altar of Burnt Offering. If we look we can see, that they are prototypes of better things to come, they are types and shadows of a more perfect way.

Let's look at the Sanctuary in Exodus 25:8-9, "They are to make me a Sanctuary, that I may live among them. You are to make it according to everything I show you – the design of the Tabernacle and the design of its furnishings. This is how you are to make it." Notice, this is all by God's design. Amen.

The sanctuary, in Hebrew "#4720 Miqqedesh a sacred place, holy place," "#4908 Mishcan a Tabernacle," a place where the Lord may dwell among men. Can we see Yeshua in the Tabernacle? Yes, Hebrews 9:11, "But Christ came as High Priest of the good things to come, with the greater and more perfect tabernacle not made with hands, that is, not of this creation." Amen. Know that the Holy spirit dwells within you, when you accept Jesus Christ as your Savior and Lord (Romans 8:11).

The Ark of the Covenant, in Hebrew "#727 Aron and 5715 Eduth, literally, Ark of Testimony, container of the Word," Jesus is the Word of God, (John 1:1-4). The Ark contains the Tablets of the 10 Commandments, a jar of Manna, the Rod of Aaron and the Mercy Seat sits on top. The 10 Commandments, God's judgments "Mishpatim #4941." Jesus is that judgment, only through Him are our sins forgiven (John 5:24).

The jar of Manna? Manna In Hebrew meaning "what is it?" Moses explained, "it is bread God has given" (Exodus 16:15). That's God's provision. Jesus is that provision, only through Him are we promised to be provided for eternally (2 Thessalonians 2:16) and Jesus is the Bread of Life (John 6:41-50).

The Rod of Aaron "#4294 mattah," is a symbol of authority and priesthood. Jesus is that authority, He is that priesthood (Hebrews 8:26).

The Mercy Seat is "#3727 kapporeth" in Hebrew, but it also means "the price of life." Yeshua Messiah is the Mercy Seat because, only through Him can we find salvation. By grace we are saved (Ephesians 2:3-10). Yes, Jesus is the Ark, He gave His life as our ransom price (Mark 10:45)

They built the Table of the Showbread. In Hebrew "Shulchan #7979 Lechem #3899 Panim #6440" Yeshua, Jesus is the Show-bread, John 6:48-51 reads, "I am the bread of life. Your fathers ate the manna in the wilderness, and are dead. This is the bread which comes down from heaven, that one may eat of it and not die. I am the living bread which came down from heaven. If anyone eats of this bread, he will live forever; and the bread that I shall give is My flesh, which I shall give for the life of the world." Yes, yes, yes, Jesus is the table for the showbread.

They made the Golden Lampstand. In Hebrew "Zahab #2091 Menorah #4501" this is recorded in John 8:12, "Then Jesus spoke to them again, saying, "I am the light of the world. He who fol-lows Me shall not walk in darkness, but have the light of life."

They made the Burning Altar. In Hebrew "Mizbeakh #4196." Jesus is that altar, only through Him can we be made wholly acceptable to Elohim as a sweet savor rising from the puri-fying flames of His righteousness, John the Baptist testifies of Him in Matthew 3:11. "I indeed baptize you with water unto repentance, but He who is coming after me is mightier than I, whose sandals I am not worthy to carry. He will baptize you with the Holy Spirit and fire." Amen, that is what the "Terumah" offerings then, did for us now.

Haftarah Portion
1 Kings 5:26-6:13

From the Prophet's reading, the Haftarah in 1 Kings 5:12, we see the Lord give Solomon wisdom in the building of the Temple by making peace with Hiram, King of Tyre and gaining access to the forests of Lebanon, the renowned Cedars of Lebanon "#730 erez." to make beams, boards and paneling from. Thus the Temple was beautified.

Of only hundreds of Erez trees left in Lebanon, there are examples of them being 8 to 12 feet in diameter and 120 to 130 feet tall, comparable say, to the redwoods in California. I can only imagine that in biblical times there might have been trees as big as the giant sequoias.

King Solomon had the most beautiful, lavish, costly structures built that had ever been constructed before. Even the pyramids pale in comparison as they are in reality, just a big pile of rock with a few tiny rooms in them.

Moses built the Tabernacle, the cost being almost incalculable by today's standards. The Menorah alone was made with one talent of pure gold. One talent is about 70 pounds, or about $3 million in today's dollars. They used around a ton, 2,000 pounds of pure gold in that tent "mishkan," 7,000 pounds of silver and 5,000 pounds of bronze. Possibly a billion-dollar tent, wow! I can hardly imagine.

God dwelt among men, in the pillar of cloud by day and pillar of fire by night, and all Moses had to do to talk with God was stand before the Ark of the Covenant. Really, God wants to be with His people.

Solomon built the Temple as a dwelling place for God, sparing no expense. God dwelt among men. The Temple in today's money would cost in the trillions of dollars not billions. As the construction progressed, the Lord reminded Solomon that what really mattered was not the Temple, built with the finest cedar, stone, gold and silver, but keeping God's statutes, the 10 Commandments and the law. When it comes to building a temple for God, it is not the size, beauty or expense of the Temple, but the free will, heartfelt attitudes of those who build and come to worship in that Temple. Think about it, God does not dwell in a temple made by human hands anymore, He dwells in the people building the Temple. First Corinthians 3:16-17 reads, "Do you not know that you are the temple of God. And that the Spirit of God dwells in you? If anyone defiles the temple of God, God will destroy him. For the temple of God is Holy, which temple are you?" Amen. The best offering "Terumah" we can make to the Lord is to serve Him willingly.

God does not need our "Terumah" offering. Everything we have comes from Him anyway. Our one true sacrifice to Him then would be our irredeemable time that we spend in worship. The time we spend in praise and joyous service to Him is really our only true offering, sacrifice, "Terumah", Amen. So let your worship and praise time be unto the Lord, and let yourself and your life be the "Terumah" you lift up before Him.

Gospel Portion
Matthew 12:46-13:58

Our readings from the Gospel Portion in Matthew 12:46-13:58 show us Yeshua, Jesus as He uses parables to teach, not only His disciples, but all who will listen, how to approach God with the right heart and mind attitudes.

God desires not just that we sacrifice to Him, but that we come to Him with Thanksgiving. He wants us to come into His Kingdom with no reservations. Jesus teaches us that our faith in Him is the only way to Heaven, but our obedience to God, His precepts and Commandments will bring great reward in this life and the next. Amen.

Parable after parable shows us God's grace, God's mercy, God's love and God's reward. They are just shadows of things to come. If you make your life a "Terumah" offering to Him, sacrificing your time, your talents and your energies you will receive so much more.

"Look to yourselves, that we do not lose those things we worked for, but that we may receive a full reward." (2 John 1:8)

"And behold, I am coming quickly, and My reward is with Me, to give to everyone according to his work. I am the Alpha and the Omega, the beginning and the end, the first and the last." Blessed are those who do His commandments, that they may have the right to the tree of life, and may enter through the gates into the city." (Revelation 22:12-14)

From GOD through Moses to YOU

Amen. Yes, there is a city being built, the new Jerusalem, where there is no temple, for the Lord God Almighty and the Lamb are its temple (Revelation 21:22). Now that will be glorious!

Would you like to give yourself to God as an offering? It's as easy as ABC.

    A. Admit, admit you have sinned and ask forgiveness for those sins.
    B. Believe, believe Jesus died for those sins, then rose from the grave on the third day.
    C. Confess, confess Jesus is Lord and make Him King in your life.

Read John 3:16-21 and Romans 10:8-13, then pray a prayer of repentance and ask that Father God accept your life as a living sacrifice and that He will fill you with His Holy Spirit. Pray in Jesus' Name, Amen.

If you prayed that prayer, I would like to welcome you to the family of God. I would also like to encourage you to tell a Pastor, Messianic Rabbi or Christian friend, they will know what to do next. You can contact us here at jewandgentileministries.org.

Bibliography for Terumah "offerings"
Interlinear Bible, The, Hendrickson publishing, 2006
New King James Version of the Bible, Thomas Nelson publishers, 2007
Strong's Complete Dictionary of the Bible Words, Thomas Nelson publishing, 1996

Tetzaveh

"you shall command"

Exodus 27:20-30:10
Ezekiel 43:10-27
Mark 4:35-5:43

This Torah study titled "Tetzaveh," in Hebrew means "you shall command," teaches us that if we read, study and meditate on God's precepts law and Scripture, we can act with authority to command God's Word.

Additional Scripture

Isaiah 53:1-12

Malachi 4:2

Matthew 7:29, 28:18

Philippians 2:9

2 Timothy 3:16-17

Acts 17:30-31

Matthew 3:7

Romans 10:8-13

Colossians 3:17

From GOD through Moses to YOU

This Torah Portion titled "Tetzaveh #6680" in Hebrew means "you shall command." It is found in exodus 27:20-30:10.

Exodus 27:20 records a statute to always care for the Menorah.

Exodus 28:1-14 records making garments for the priesthood.

Exodus 28:15 records the making of the Breastplate of Judgment.

Exodus 28:31 records making the robe of the Ephod all of blue.

Exodus 29:1 records Aaron and his sons being consecrated to the priesthood.

Exodus 29:38 records the daily offerings.

Exodus 30:1-10 records plans for making the Altar of Incense.

The Haftarah or Prophets' Portion is in Ezekiel 43:10-27

Ezekiel 43:10-27 records God commanding Ezekiel to make known the design of the Temple and its arrangement to the Israelites.

The Gospel Portion is in Mark 4:35-5:43

Mark 4:35 records Jesus stilling the water.

Mark 5:1 records Yeshua casts demons out of a man.

Mark 5:21 records Jairus pleading for his daughter..

Mark 5:25 records the woman with the issue of blood is healed.

Mark 5:35 records that Jairus' daughter is healed.

Tetzaveh "you shall command"

Torah Portion
Exodus 27:20-30:10

We find the word for our Torah Portion title in Exodus 27:20 (Interlinear Bible). "And you shall command "#6680 Tetzaveh" the sons of Israel and let them bring to you olive oil beaten for the light. To set up lamps perpetually."

God says to Moses, "you shall "command, Tetzaveh" the children of Israel." God gave authority to Moses to command the children of Israel to bring offerings of pure oil, and to instruct them in the making of the Tabernacle, priestly garments, Ephod, Breastplate, Altars, Menorah, and all the furnishings of the Sanctuary and the Ark of the Testimony.

Why was it important to know all that stuff? Because to know it is to own it. To own something is to have authority, "command" over it, and how to utilize it for its intended purpose. When something is used for its intended purpose it produces the best results.

Offerings "Terumah #8641" of olive oil were used for anointing the Priests and Levites (then later kings). Olive oil was used for fuel in the Menorah, for balms and salves, for food preparation and lubrication.

Instruction on the making and layout of the Tabernacle was important because, in the layout we see the pattern of the cross, from the East we see the Altar of burnt Offering, then the Bronze Lavor. To the North we see the Table of Showbread, to the South the gold Menorah, to the West the Altar of Incense and beyond the Altar of Incense, is the Holy of Holies, God's presence, showing our need to pass through the cross to get to God's presence, Amen. We see there's no other way than by the narrow path (Matthew 7:13).

Exodus 28 records the making of the priestly garments. When they were clothed in their *priestly garments: robe, fringes, ephod, breastplate* and all, they were identified to God and of God.

When we wear the Tallit, fringes, we are identified by the world as being with or belonging to God. When instructed on the Ephod, Breastplate, Urim and Thummim, we understand it is possible to communicate with God. Though these ancient artifacts have long since vanished, we know we can communicate with God through prayer.

The Altars, the gold Menorah and all the furnishings of the Sanctuary teach us we are to present ourselves as acceptable sacrifices to the Lord. We are to be lights in the darkness of this world and also that we, like all the different furnishings and utensils, being different yet the same, all have a purpose in God's Kingdom. Amen.

When we are instructed on the Ark of the Testimony, we begin to understand the power of God's Word. In the Ark we find the tablets of the 10 Commandments, the Testaments, the Scripture. Then you understand the authority we've been given in Gods Word, the Scriptures, to "Tetztaveh" command, to speack over the circumstances of our lives. If we speak God's will into this earth, if we speak scripturally, God's Word will not return to Him void (Isaiah 55:11). That's the power and authority God invests into His children to command.

When you have command of the Word of God, the Scripture, it will go forth and produce the effect it was intended for. "All Scripture is given by inspiration of God, and is profitable for doctrine, for reproof, for correction, for instruction in righteousness, that the man of God be complete, thoroughly equipped for every good work" (2 Timothy 3:16-17). Learn to Tetzaveh "command" the Word of God.

Haftarah Portion
Ezekiel 43:10-20

Ezekiel 43:10-20 reads, "son of man, describe the Temple to the house of Israel, that they may be ashamed of their iniquities; and let them measure the pattern, and if they are ashamed of all that they have done, make known to them the design of the Temple and its arrangement, its exits and its entrances, its entire design and all its ordinances, all its forms and all its laws. Write it down in their sight, so that they may keep its whole design and all its ordinances, and perform them."

God commands "Tetzaveh" Ezekiel to instruct the people on the design and arrangement of the Temple. It's the same pattern as the Tabernacle. You still have to abide by the laws, statutes and ordinances. The furnishings are the same, so you would still need to pass through the cross, through the middle wall of separation, the narrow way, to get to the Holy of Holies. We learned in last week's Torah Portion that the Tabernacle and all the furnishings were types and shadows, representations of the

Messiah, Yeshua; and only through Him can we hope to find eternal salvation, abiding with Elohim.

Gospel Portion
Mark 4:35-5:43

In Mark 4:39 Yeshua, Jesus commands "Tetzaveh" the winds to be still.

In Mark 5:8 Jesus commands the unclean spirit to come out of a man.

In Mark 5:19 Jesus commands the man to go, "Go to your people and testify to what the Lord has done for you, and how He has had compassion on you."

Here, Yeshua is in essence telling the Gadarenes, Greeks from one of the cities of the Decapolis, and all the people that were with Him, that He was God. Yeshua, Jesus does a miracle before these pagan Greeks, who were considered by the Jews to be unclean because they ate pork and worshiped many different idols. Yeshua, Jesus, God reveals Himself to an unclean people, in an unclean place, a swine herd by a graveyard. He does a great wonder before them and still, they fear Him and not just ask Him but beg Him to leave. It just boggles my mind that they, or anybody, could reject Him.

Jesus has the power and authority. He could have just commanded that they worship Him, but no, He let them choose, just as He let the demons choose. Jesus didn't command the demons to leave the man and go into the pigs, they asked and He let them go, despite knowing it would lead to their ultimate destruction.

Tetzaveh "you shall command"

Jesus didn't command them to go, He let them go. See, commanding is a form of judgment and it was not yet time to judge. God gives everyone the choice to serve Him or not. The alcoholic, the drug addict, the sexually immoral, they all choose their way and God lets them go, even though He knows it will lead to their ultimate destruction, and if they do not repent, they have chosen Hell.

We see Yeshua command and miracles happen. I get it, He's the Son of God. He speaks God's will into the earth scripturally because He is that Scripture, the Word in flesh.

"In the beginning was the Word, and the Word was with God, and the Word was God. He was in the beginning with God." (John 1:1-2)

We have been authorized to use the Name above all names, Jesus, Yeshua, Amen.

"Therefore God also has highly exalted Him and given Him the name which is above every name, that at the name of Jesus every knee should bow, of those in heaven, and of those on earth, and of those under the earth, and that every tongue should confess that Jesus Christ is Lord, to the glory of God the Father." (Philippians 2:9-11)

"And whatever you do in word or deed, do all in the name of the Lord Jesus, giving thanks to God the Father through Him." (Colossians 3:17)

As was said in our Torah study, we can, we should, use Scripture, the Word of God to speak into and over all circumstances in our lives. Let's consider now the woman with the issue of blood in Mark 5:25. Her issue by itself made her unclean. She wasn't even supposed to be in public, yet she dared to touch a Rabbi, why? What could make the sick woman chance such a brazen act? Hope? Determination? No, I believe it was much more than that. I think she knew a particular passage of Scripture, that she would have heard in the synagogue since she was a child. Malachi 4:2 and this is embroidered in one corner of my Tallit. "But to you who fear My name The Sun of Righteousness shall arise with healing in His wings."

It was not hope that drove her that day, I believe she recognized Him as Messiah, as Yeshua Ha Mashiach "#4886 the anointed," and she reached out and took hold of the wings, the fringe of His garment the "tsitsith #6734." I believe she knew the Scriptures well enough, had command of enough Scripture, to reach out in faith, believing He was Who He said He was.

"And He said to her, "daughter your faith has made you well. "Go in peace, and be healed of your affliction" (Mark 5:34). You too can develop that kind of faith to command by reading and meditating on the Word of God.

In Mark 5:21, we see Yeshua being stopped by Jairus to ask that He come heal his daughter. Jairus #2971 meaning "enlightener," was a ruler at the local synagogue and more than likely taught Torah. Anyway, as it happened, on His way to heal the man's daughter, He was delayed by the woman with the issue of blood and so the daughter dies. As soon as Jesus heard the word that was spoken, He tells Jairus: "Do not be afraid; only believe." Yeshua does not say "just believe in me," "or just believe I can raise her from the dead." Yeshua is telling him to believe in what he has studied and taught most of his life, the Torah, the Scriptures, the Prophets!

Especially, what the Prophet Isaiah said in chapter 53, all of it.

Again, embroidered here on another corner of my Tallit is Isaiah 53:5. "But He was wounded for our transgressions, He was bruised for our iniquities; the chastisement for our peace was upon Him, and by His stripes we are healed." Amen, Jesus told Jairus to take command, to stand, to believe on the Scriptures he had taught and command the Word of God!

Through the story, the Greek word for "child," "#3813 paidion" is used three times. So, why change the words to "Talitha Cumi?" Well, if we look at the Jewishness or the Hebraic side of the story (as all participants in the story were Hebrew), we find that in Jewish tradition it is customary to cover the dead with a Talit, (prayer shawl from #2926 and 6734 tassels) while waiting for burial and even to bury the dead in their Talit. So, Yeshua didn't say "girl arise," He said, "arise one covered by the Talit," "Talit ha qumi" as the Greek word "kumi #2891" and Hebrew word "qum #6965" both mean to "arise."

We can further look at the scriptural significance of this miracle when we consider that, the woman with the issue of blood reached out and took hold of Yeshua's Talit tassel and Jairus' daughter was covered by a Talit with tsitsith on the corners, representing the sacred Name YHVH, the 619 laws given to Moses, the Word of God and the 10 Commandments of God. Amen.

"O Jerusalem, Jerusalem, the one who kills the prophets and stones those who were sent to her! How often I wanted to gather your children together, as a hen gathers her chicks under her wings, but you were not willing!" (Matthew 23:37)

This is a perfect illustration of Jesus wanting to wrap all of humanity in His Talit.

In Matthew 3:17b, Yeshua gives a command "Tetzaveh," "Repent, for the Kingdom of Heaven is at hand." Do not doubt that we are all commanded to repent. Acts 17:30 reads, "Truly, these times of ignorance God overlooked, but now commands "Tetzaveh" all men everywhere to repent, because He has appointed a day on which He will judge the world in righteousness by the Man who He has ordained. He has given assurance of this to all by raising Him from the dead." Amen.

People, beloved of the Father, when God the Father is presented with His Word, He will do nothing else but fulfill it and be moved by it. Learn to "Tetzaveh" command the Scriptures, to line your life up with God's will. His will is for you to come to salvation through His Son Jesus. If you want this in your life, it's as easy to command as ABC.

A. Admit, admit you have sinned and repent of them.
B. Believe, believe Jesus died for that sin, and rose from the grave on the third day.
C. Confess, confess with your mouth that Jesus is Lord and make Him King in your life.

Tetzaveh "you shall command"

Read Romans 10:8-13 and John 3:16 then pray asking forgiveness, confessing Jesus and asking the Father to fill you with His Holy Spirit and begin to command the Scripture. When you're done, tell a Pastor, Messianic Rabbi, Christian friend or us at jewandgentileministries.org

---

Bibliography for Tetzaveh "you shall command"
Interlinear Bible, The Hendrickson publishing, 2006
New King James Version of the Bible, Thomas Nelson publishers, 2007
Strong's Complete Dictionary of the Bible Words, Thomas Nelson publishing, 1996

NOTES:

NOTES:

Ki Tisa
"when you lift"

Exodus 30:11-34:35
1 Kings 18:1-39
Matthew 9:35-11:1

This Torah study titled "Ki Tisa" in Hebrew means "when you lift." It teaches us that we no longer have to pay the ransom money for our lives. We learn that Jesus, Yeshua has paid that price once for all, with His own precious blood, obtaining eternal redemption for all who turn to Him.

Additional Scripture

Hebrews 8:25, 9:11-15   Isaiah 53:12
Matthew 10:32   John 1:3
Colossians 2:2-3

From GOD through Moses to YOU

The Torah Portion titled "KI Tisa" in Hebrew is found in Exodus 30:11-34:10

Exodus 30:11 records that every man shall give a ransom for himself.

Exodus 30:17 records the plans for the Bronze Laver.

Exodus 30:22 records the recipe for the Holy Anointing oil.

Exodus 30:34 records the recipe for the Holy Incense.

Exodus 31:1 records leaders chosen to build the Tabernacle.

Exodus 31:12 records the Sabbath law explained.

Exodus 32 records Israel's idolatry with the golden calf.

Exodus 33:1 records the Lord commanding Israel to leave Sinai.

Exodus 33:7 records Moses meeting with the Lord.

Exodus 33:12 records the promise of God's presence.

Exodus 34:1 records Moses making new tablets of stone.

Exodus 34:10 records the renewal of the covenant.

The Haftarah or Prophets' Portion is in 1 Kings 18:1-39

1 Kings 18 records Elijah's message to Ahab and the victory on Mount Caramel.

The Gospel Portion is in Matthew 9:35-11:1

Matthew 9:35, records Jesus praying for laborers in His harvest.

Matthew 10 records the twelve Apostles being instructed and sent to preach, heal and raise the dead.

Ki Tisa "when you lift"

Torah Portion
Exodus 30:11-34:35

Exodus 30:11 (Interlinear Bible) is where we get the title "Ki Tisa" to our Torah study today. This is one I am still researching. I understand "Ki #3588 to mean "when or for" but, "Tisa" being translated as "nasa #5375" puzzles me. Ideas? jewandgentileministries.org

Vayahdabar YHVH elMoshe laamar kitisa et rosh beni yisrael. "And Jehovah spoke to Moses, saying: when you lift up the head of the sons of Israel" (Exodus 30:11-12a Interlinear Bible).

"The Lord spoke to Moses, saying: when you take the census of the children of Israel." Basically, when you count them. Anyway, once a year, those who were counted among the children of Israel, were required to give an offering to the Lord, a ransom for himself, rich or poor, you paid a half shekel per year for your life, for redemption." (Exodus 30:11-12a)

When I was in Israel the exchange rate was four shekels to the dollar, so a half shekel was worth 12 ½ cents. Even in Moses' day it was not very much. On Yom Kippur, the day of atonement, the Levite Priests would sacrifice bulls, goats and sheep. Blood would have to be spilled to make propitiation for sin, to make them at one with God again, and again, and again. The Priests and Levites would stand to make intercession for them, year after year, not so now. Hebrews 8:25 reads, "Therefore He is also able to save to the uttermost those who come to God through Him, since He always lives to make intercession for them." And Hebrews 9:12 reads, "not of goats and calves, but with His own blood He entered the Most Holy Place once for all, having obtained eternal redemption." Amen.

Yeshua did "Ki Tisa" lift up, count, redeem us. He paid the ultimate price.

In Exodus 30:17, the Lord spoke to Moses saying, "you shall also make a laver of bronze, for washing." This was symbolic of their continuous need to be washed from sin. We, those who have accepted Jesus as Savior, no longer need this ceremonial rite, as Jesus is the Bronze Laver.

"But when the kindness and the love of God our Savior toward man appeared, not by works of righteousness which we have done, but according to His mercy He saved us, through the washing of regeneration and renewing of the Holy Spirit, whom He poured out on us abundantly through Jesus Christ our Savior." (Titus 3:4-5)

In Exodus 30:23-33 the Lord spoke to Moses, saying in verse 25a, "and you shall make from these a holy anointing oil." Though costly, and I would assume having a very pleasant aroma, the holy anointing oil was still part of a works-based religion.

"And walk in love, as Christ also has loved us and given Himself for us, and offering and a sacrifice to God for a sweet smelling aroma" (Ephesians 5:2). Amen.

In Exodus 31:1-11, the Lord spoke to Moses, choosing Bezalel and appointing Aholiab in all manner of workmanship and wisdom that they make all that had been commanded made for the Tabernacle of Meeting. Colossians 2:2-3 says, "that their hearts may be encouraged, being knit together in love, and attaining to all riches of the full assurance of understanding, to the knowledge of the mystery of God, both of the Father and of Christ, in whom are hidden all the treasures of wisdom and knowledge."

"All things were made through Him, and without Him nothing was made that was made." (John 1:3)

Exodus 31:12, Sabbath regulations, Jesus is the Sabbath (Matthew 11:28-30).

In Exodus 32, the people and Aaron make a golden calf, an idol, after they thought Moses was delayed from coming down the mountain. I really don't get the mindset of the people when all they had to do was look out their tent flaps to the pillar of cloud by day and the pillar of fire by night and see that God was there among them. Or in this case look toward the top of Mount Sinai and behold the Shekinah glory as it enshrouded the mountain. There is a whole sermon here, but it just makes me sad.

"Because, although they knew God, they did not glorify Him as God, nor were thankful, but became futile in their thoughts, and their foolish hearts were darkened. Professing to be wise, they became fools, and changed the glory of the incorruptible God into an image made like corruptible man – and birds and four-footed animals and creeping things." (Romans 1:21-23)

From GOD through Moses to YOU

In Exodus 33, the Lord commands the children of Israel to leave the Sinai, then Moses meets with the Lord and God promises Moses and the children of Israel, "My presence will go with you and I will give you rest" (Exodus 33:14). Compare Matthew 11:28-30

In Exodus 34, Moses makes new stone tablets for the 10 Commandments, then delivers them to the people and the covenant is renewed. And as a reminder for the golden calf incident, God, refers to Himself in Exodus 34:14-17 as a "jealous God #7065 El Qanah".

James 4:4 reads, "Do you not know that friendship with the world is enmity with God? Whoever therefore wants to be a friend of the world makes himself an enemy of God. Or do you not think that the Scripture says in vain, 'the Spirit who dwells in us yearns jealously'? But He gives more grace therefore He says: God resists the proud, but gives grace to the humble."

Exodus 34:29-35 ends our Torah Portion this week with a curious addendum. It records that Moses' face would shine after he talked with God. I am sure this was a sign that God counted Moses worthy to guide Israel and (nisa) lifted him up as an example for all of Israel to see. Compare this to Matthew 17:2, Jesus' face did shine like the sun!

Haftarah Portion
1 Kings 18:1-39

1 Kings 18 records the story of Elijah as he contends with the

false prophets and defeats them. If we look deeper into the story we can see the underlying truths that are revealed.

Following King Ahab's example, the children of Israel sin against God by worshiping idols and participating in the abominable rites they all seem to demand. So Elijah, directed of God, pronounces a drought on the land that lasts three years, during which time Jezebel, Ahab's wife, massacres the Priests and Prophets of God. Then the Lord sends Elijah to King Ahab to set things right.

We see in the story that Elijah has Ahab call the children of Israel to Mount Caramel. Mount Caramel overlooks the Jezreel #3157 valley, "Har Magedon #717 Greek", which we call Armageddon, the valley of judgment for the nations that come against Israel at the end of the age. So, Elijah calls the nation of Israel to a place of judgment, there he kills the bull for a sacrifice of blood before the Lord as it would be for atonement, for the propitiation of sin, for their redemption. He paid the ransom for their lives by interceding on their behalf. Amen.

This is not the only place we see Elijah as a type of Christ. He also emulates Jesus, Yeshua in that he influenced the weather, i.e., the drought. By God's Word, he multiplied the food stores of the widow woman that it should not run out before the drought was over. He raises the widow's son from death, he went into the wilderness for 40 days and he ascends into Heaven when his ministry was at end. Amen. Again, God provides a way of redemption for them.

Jesus stilled the wind (Mark 4:39). He fed the 5000 with five loaves and two fishes (Matthew 14:13). Jesus raises the dead back to life (Matthew 9:18) Yeshua went into the wilderness 40 days to be tempted (Matthew 4:1). He ascended up into Heaven and sat down at the right hand of God (Mark 16:19). When you lift up "Ki Tisa," your prayers, He, our living Lord, is there to receive them, unlike the dead, deaf and dumb idols so many seem to revere in this fallen world's religious systems. I pray for the souls of those enslaved by Hinduism, Buddhism and Catholicism, may Jesus Christ reveal Himself to them and set them free, Amen.

Gospel Portion
Matthew 9:35-11:1

In Matthew 9:35, Jesus asks His disciples to pray the Lord of the harvest "#3068 and 7114 YHVH Qatsar" to send out laborers into His harvest, that they may count, redeem, and lift up "Ki Tisa" the unsaved, the lost, the hurting of this world, that they would repent and be brought into the Kingdom of Heaven (Matthew 4:17).

Now, we don't have to have Priests redeem us. We don't have to have Prophets redeem us. We don't even need Apostles to redeem us. We don't have to redeem ourselves anymore. We don't have to make atonement once a year for our propitiation. We don't have to save, make or find the money, even the half shekel, to pay our ransom to the Lord. It's been paid when we repent of our sins and call Jesus Lord! But Yeshua does tell us to count the cost of our discipleship, and yes, you are all disciples of Christ. In Matthew 10:16 it says, "Behold, I send you out as sheep in the midst of wolves. Therefore, be wise as serpents and harmless as doves. But beware of men, for they will deliver you up "Ki Tisa" to councils and scourge you in their synagogues."

We all will or have, paid a price for our faith. We've all been tested and tried. Some have paid a small sum (half shekel), others a great price. For some it is just giving up the distractions of this world. For others, it cost them their families, wives, sons, daughters, mothers or fathers, friends and position in the community. Then there are those who are called to give all in this world, the ultimate price, the life of their bodies. Know this, we will all have to count the cost in one way or another.

I won't tell you that if you give your life to Christ all your troubles will just disappear, because that would be a lie. A lot of the time when you start to live for Jesus, your old master, Satan, gets upset and comes against you in all manner of ways. Satan hates us, he comes only to kill, steal and destroy (John 10:10). When we live a sin-filled life, Satan doesn't pay much attention because he knows we are already headed for Hell.

But, when you confess and believe Jesus as Lord in your life, Satan will come against you; and if this body is the price we have to pay, well so be it, because we now have that blessed promise of life eternal in Jesus Yeshua. Amen.

"And it is appointed for men to die once. But after this the judgment, so Christ was offered once to bear the sins of many. To those who eagerly wait for Him He will appear a second time, apart from sin, for salvation." (Hebrews 9:27-28)

From GOD through Moses to YOU

Jesus paid the ransom price for that life, for us by shedding His blood, every last drop, on Calvary.

People, beloved of God, if you are ready to receive the free gift of salvation it's as easy as ABC.

A. Admit, admit you have sinned and ask forgiveness.
B. Believe, believe Jesus died for that sin, then rose from the grave on the third day.
C. Confess, confess with your mouth that Jesus is Lord and make Him King in your life.

Read Matthew 10:32 and John 3:15-18. Then pray for Father God to fill you with His Holy Spirit so you can " Ki Tisa" be counted among the redeemed. Pray in Jesus' Name, Amen.

If you prayed that prayer, I would like to welcome you to the family of God, and encourage you to go tell a Pastor, Messianic Rabbi, a Christian friend or email us here at jewandgentileministries.org. Shalom.

Bibliography for Ki Tisa "when you lift"
Interlinear Bible, The Hendrickson publishing, 2006
New King James Version of the Bible, Thomas Nelson publishers, 2007
Strong's Complete Dictionary of the Bible Words, Thomas Nelson publishing, 1996

Vaya'qhal

"and assembled"

Exodus 35:1-38:20
1 Kings 7:40
Ezekiel 36:24-29
Mark 6:14-29

This Torah study, titled "Vaya'qhal" in Hebrew means "and assembled" or "and gathered," teaches us first, the Sabbath regulations. Then we learn about the making of the Tabernacle. The Tabernacle's beautiful furnishings, made with precious materials in Moses' and Solomon's time, teach us how precious God deems His new Temple, that Temple is you.

Additional Scripture

Genesis 3:8	John 2:21
Deuteronomy 29:5	1 Corinthians 3:9-17
1 Kings 8:10	2 Corinthians 6:11-18
Isaiah 7:14	1 Timothy 2:3-6
Matthew 5:14-16	

From GOD through Moses to YOU

The Torah Portion titled "Vaya'qhal" this week is in Exodus 35:1-38:20

Exodus 35:1 records Moses assembling the children of Israel together.

Exodus 35:4 records that the children of Israel were required to give an offering for the building and the furnishings of the Tabernacle, so an offering was presented and the workmen were recognized.

Exodus 36:1 records that the people gave more than enough to build the Tabernacle.

Exodus 37 records the making of the Ark of the Testimony, Table for the Showbread, the gold Menorah, the Altar of Incense, the Anointing oil and the incense.

Exodus 38 records making the Altar of Burnt Offering and the Bronze Laver.

The Haftarah or Prophets' Portion is in 1 Kings 7:40-50 and Ezekiel 36:24-29

1 Kings 7:40-50 records the furnishings for the Temple.

Ezekiel 36:24-29 records God writing the new covenant in man's heart.

The Gospel Portion is in Mark 6:14-29

Mark 6:14-29 records the murder of John the Baptist.

Vaya'qhal "and assembled"

Torah Study
Exodus 35:1-38:20

This week's Torah study titled "Vaya'qhal #6950" means "and assembled" in Hebrew.

Exodus 35:1 (Interlinear Bible) reads, "and Moses assembled "Vaya'qhal #6950" all the congregation of the sons of Israel and said to them, these are the words which Jehovah has commanded, to do them."

Moses assembled the congregation of Israel to take up free-will offerings of all manner of material for the building of the Tabernacle and its furnishings.

Okay, let's contemplate the Tabernacle. To start with, why did God need a tent? To keep Him out of the weather? No, did God need a place to sleep after a hard day's work? No, or did God need a place to keep all His neat stuff? No, why then make this large, expensive tent or Tabernacle?

Because, God, Yahweh, wanted to be near His chosen people. God wanted to live among His people and establish an intimate relationship with them. Since the beginning, in the Garden of Eden, God made man for fellowship. God would walk with Adam and talk with him in the cool of the day (Genesis 3:8). Then, as now, God wants/desires to be with us. The Garden of Eden was the first outworking of that desire.

The Hebrew word for Tabernacle "Mishkan #4908," meaning "a dwelling place," is from the primary root word "shakan #7931" meaning, "dwell, inhabit, nest, to settle down or to live among."

From GOD through Moses to YOU

This is the second outworking of Gods desire for relationship.

The third outworking of that desire would be Solomon's Temple, the fourth outworking of that desire was Yeshua, Jesus, God becoming a man, as the Son of God. Yeshua lived among us, walked among us and revealed God the Father to us. This is why His Name is "Immanuel #6005" meaning "God with us" (Isaiah 7:14), and the ultimate outworking of God's desire to live with us is now to live in each and every one of us! Galatians 2:20 reads, "I have been crucified with Christ; it is no longer I who live, but Christ lives in me; and the life which I now live in the flesh I live by the faith of the Son of God." Amen.

Let's go back and consider the Tabernacle from a human standpoint. It was utterly spectacular, so richly adorned and artistically apportioned that there had not been anything like it before or since. Made with gold, silver and bronze, expensive skins and furs, fabrics of blue, purple and scarlet thread, fine acacia wood, anointed with pure olive oil and perfumed with sweet smelling incense, it must have been a glory to behold!

Gold was for divinity. Silver represents purity. Bronze signifies strength and fidelity. The color blue was for virtue. The color purple represents royalty. The scarlet color signifies sacredness. The acacia wood represents the flesh and was covered in gold, symbolizing God's divine grace.

The completed Tabernacle and court used an estimated one ton, 2,000 pounds of gold. The amount of silver, a staggering 7,000 pounds, came from just the men over age 20. The men brought a half shekel of silver each, the ransom sum appointed for the service of the Tabernacle (Exodus 30:12). This was collected of the men from the 12 tribes that came out of Egypt, 603,550 men over age 20, all giving about a dime's worth of silver.

They also used about 5,000 pounds, or 2 ½ half tons of bronze.

The cost today would be over $100 million, now that was some tent!

The Tabernacle of the Lord was used from the time of Moses until the time of King Solomon, that's twelve generations, or 480 years (1 Kings 6:1). God's Holy presence was in the Ark of the Tabernacle. God dwelled among men all that time. Did God's divine presence sustain that tent miraculously from decay, wear and age? I think so, it is recorded that the children of Israel's sandals did not wear out during 40 years in the wilderness (Deuteronomy 29:5) so God's Tabernacle could last 500 years, right? I don't know of any passage of Scripture where one Priest or king ordered a new cover for the sanctuary because the old one was just too shabby, Amen! It's also recorded that all the furnishings, Ark, Menorah Altars and utensils were taken into the Temple in Jerusalem after it was completed. Then, God's presence, God's glory, His Shekinah filled that Temple.

As expensive as the old tabernacle was, the new Temple was even grander, on the scale of about 100 times over, as recorded through first and second Kings and first and second Chronicles. The materials amassed for the first Temple by Solomon was 5,000 talents of gold, 10,000 derricks of gold, 1,017,000 talents of silver, I didn't do the math, but I would assume that's billions of dollars today. Wow, staggering. That's a lot of money. Now think about this, the next time God chose to dwell among men, He came in the form of flesh as the man, Yeshua Messiah, Jesus. Matthew 12:6 records Jesus' Words. "Yet I say to you that in this place there is One greater than the Temple." And in John 2:19, "Jesus answered and said to them, 'destroy this temple, and in three days I will raise it up.' But, He was speaking of His body."

God's only begotten Son, the Holy Temple of God, God incarnate on Earth, Immanuel, God with us, became the ransom price for our sin. His precious blood was the ransom price to be used in the service and making of the new Tabernacle of God. First was the Tabernacle, second was the Temple, third was Jesus, and forth the new dwelling place of God, you and me. The new Temple on Earth, that most costly, precious, Holy Temple, is you and you and you.

Think about it, you are the new Temples of God. You were made to house the Holy Spirit of God, just take a look at 1 Corinthians 3:11-16.

"For no other foundation can anyone lay than that which is laid, which is Jesus Christ. Now if anyone builds on this foundation with gold, silver, precious stones, wood, hay, straw, each one's work will become clear; for the day will declare it, because it will be revealed by fire; and the fire will test each one's work, of what sort it is. If anyone's work which he has built on it endures, he will receive a reward. If anyone's work is burned, he will suffer loss; but he himself will be saved, yet so as through fire. Do you not know that you are the temple of God and that the Spirit of God dwells in you? If anyone defiles the temple of God, God will destroy him. For the temple of God is holy, which temple you are."

"And what agreement has the temple of God with idols? For you are the temple of the living God. As God has said: 'I will dwell in them and walk among them. I will be their God and they shall be My people.' Therefore 'come out from among them and be separate says the Lord. Do not touch what is unclean, and I will receive you.'" (2 Corinthians 6:16-17)

Now do you get it? Do you understand that you are God's most precious and expensive Temple yet? You are priceless. God values you more than anything. Your soul is worth more to God then the riches of this whole Earth. You are worth more than the earth itself, God delays His coming at the expense of this earth, that not one soul should be lost.

"For this is good and acceptable in the sight of God our Savior, who desires all men to be saved and to come to the knowledge of the truth. For there is one God and one Mediator between God and men, the Man Jesus Christ, who gave Himself a ransom for all, to be testified in due time." (1 Timothy 2:3-6)

The ransom, not a half shekel of silver but the precious blood of Yeshua, redeems us, and so, that not one drop of that precious blood be wasted, He waits for you. Amen

Haftarah Portion
1 Kings 7:40-50; Ezekiel 36:24-29

The Prophet Ezekiel speaks about sanctification – sanctifica-

From GOD through Moses to YOU

tion is defined as setting something apart to make it clean and holy. Ezekiel 36:25 reads, "Then I will sprinkle clean water on you, and you shall be clean; I will cleanse you from all your filthiness and from all of your idols."

Ezekiel says, "I will sprinkle clean water on you," symbolizing the washing away of our sin. This is God's forgiveness based on the sacrificial blood atonement.

In 1 Kings 7:40-50, the making and furnishing of the Temple with such precious and beautiful furnishings symbolizes how we should fill the Temple of our mind with the precious things of God, His holy Scripture, and His infallible Word.

The cleansing (a type and shadow of water baptism) and furnishing of the Temple would be of no effect if it is disassociated from a heartfelt repentance, the renewing of the mind and the energizing influence of God's Holy Spirit.

Ezekiel 36:26 says, "I will give you a new heart and put a new spirit within you; I will take the heart of stone out of your flesh and give you a heart of flesh." Amen.

God can, does, and will restore us to our right state of being, which is for us to be that beautifully furnished, sanctified Temple where His Holy Spirit can reside. Where His Shekinah glory can shine forth through us. So, whether you are "qhal #6950," "assembled" together in church, or just out in public, let your Temple lights shine for all men to see!

"You are light for the world. A town built on a hill cannot be hidden. Likewise, when people light a lamp, they don't cover it with a bowl but put it on a lampstand, so that it shines for everyone in the house. In the same way, let your light shine before people, so that they may see the good things you do and praise your Father in heaven." (Matthew 5:14-16)

Gospel Portion
Mark 6:14-29

In our Gospel reading from Mark 6:14-29, we see kings, queens, princes, nobles, high officers and chief men, gathered, "Vaya'qhal" and assembled together. But they are not assembled in a godly way. They are partying, drinking and carousing. Their minds are not stayed on the righteousness of God, and under such circumstances, God's presence is not in that place or their minds, their Temples. Because the Holy Spirit is a gentleman and is offended by the lusts of the flesh, He departs. What happens when the Spirit of God is not in a place? Well, the enemy can come in. He comes only to kill, steal and destroy and that is just what happens in the story. Through the lusts of the flesh, the corruption of the mind and the vanity of unsanctified speech, a man is murdered. John the Baptist is executed.

I urge you to always keep your mind on the things of God.

"Finally, brethren, whatever things are true, whatever things are noble, whatever things are just, whatever things are pure, whatever things are lovely, whatever things are of good report, if there is any virtue and if there is anything praiseworthy – meditate on these things. The things which you learned and received and heard and saw in me, these do, and the God of Peace will be with you." (Philippians 4:8-9)

Whenever you are gathered together and assembled "Vaya'qhal" remember, you are the temple of God, let the words of your mouth be as an incense to God. Let your life so shine as to be the light, the Menorah in that Temple. Let all you do be as offerings "Terumah #8641" piled onto the altar of God. Let your Temple be filled with the presence of God continually. Amen.

People, beloved of God, do you want to be a Sanctuary for God? Do you want to be His Temple and have God's Holy Spirit live in you? Well, it's as easy as ABC.

A. Admit, admit you have sinned and repent of those sins.
B. Believe, believe Jesus died for those sins, then rose from the grave on the third day.
C. Confess, confess with your mouth that Jesus is Lord and make Him King in your life.

Read Romans 10:8-13 and John 3:15-18. Afterwards, pray, repent, then ask God to make you a Sanctuary and fill you with His Spirit. Thank Him, praying in Jesus' Name. Amen.

If you prayed that prayer tell a Pastor, Messianic Rabbi, a Christian friend or contact us here at jewandgentileministries.org

---

Bibliography for Vaya'qhal "and assembled"
Interlinear Bible, The Hendrickson publishing, 2006
New King James Version of the Bible, Thomas Nelson publishers, 2007
Strong's Complete Dictionary of the Bible Words, Thomas Nelson publishing, 1996

Pekudei

"numbered"

Exodus 38:21-40:38
2 Kings 12:1-17
John 6:1-71

This Torah study titled "Pekudei" in Hebrew means "numbered, or "accounted for inventory." The translation I like is "appointed for service". In this study we learn that God's focus is on the people, not just the articles that are in the Tabernacle. God predestined each of us for His service and purposes us to accomplish His will into this earth.

Additional Scripture

1 Samuel 2:2   Ecclesiastes 3:1
Psalm 95:1, 118:22   1 Peter 2:5, 9
Luke 20:17   Ephesians 2:10
Revelation 2:17, 20:3

From GOD through Moses to YOU

The Torah Portion "Pekudei" is in Exodus 38:21-40:38

Exodus 38:21, records the "Pekudei #6485", those accounted for service in the Tabernacle.

Exodus 39 records the making of the priestly garments, Ephod, Breastplate, other priestly garments and that the work was completed.

Exodus 40 records that the Tabernacle was completed and the Lord filled the Tabernacle with His glory.

The Haftarah or Prophets' Portion is in 2 Kings 12:1-17

2 Kings 12:1-17 records that Jehoash repairs the Temple.

The Gospel Portion is in John 6:1-71

John chapter 6, records Christ feeds the 5000, Jesus walks on the water and Jesus says, "I am the bread of life," then Yeshua is rejected by many followers and Peter professes Jesus as the Son of the living God.

Pekudei "numbered"

Torah Study
Exodus 38:21-40:38

Exodus 38:21 (Interlinear Bible) reads, "Elleh pekudei ha mishkan, mishkan eduth." "These are the numbered "Pekudei 6485" things of the Tabernacle of the Testimony.

Exodus 38:22 reads, "Bezalel the son of Uri, the son of Hur, of the tribe of Judah, made all that the Lord had commanded Moses. And with him was Aholiab the son of Ahismach, of the tribe of Dan, an engraver and designer, a weaver of blue, purple, and scarlet thread, and of fine linen."

By these words we learn that God's focus is on His chosen people, not the things of the Tabernacle only. We see that God predestined us, His chosen people, for service, He purposes us to accomplish His will in this earth.

Like the Ark, Bronze laver, Altar of Burnt Offerings, the gold Menorah, the Table of Showbread and Altar of Incense, all have a special purpose in God's plan. We also were predestined for His purposes. Ephesians 2:10 reads, "For we are His workmanship, created in Christ Jesus for good works, which God prepared beforehand that we should walk in them."

Before God laid the foundation of His heavens and Earth, God had a master plan, a blueprint if you will. Everything was thought out to the last detail, before He ever begin to build. Amen, think of it like this. God as the Master Builder, drawing up plans to make this earth says, "Ahh, and right here at this exact moment in time I'm going to need a special person named (*add your name here*), I don't have one, so I will make one of those very special and unique creatures to accomplish this or that purpose. Wow, God did not have a you, so He made a you, Ta Daaa!

In God's master plan, God's Book of Life, He has recorded the names of all His creation from before time was created, all of our names are recorded in that Great Book of life, that Master plan, of which our Bible is just a tiny fraction, the rest of the Great Book, it's pages being turned into all eternity. But back to the Bible, the names recorded there, as written in stone, like Adam, Methuselah, Enoch, Noah, Abraham, Isaac, Jacob and Moses; such well-known names, but there are many names recorded in this book that are just as important, in that they fulfilled their purpose as God intended, even if they are not mentioned as much.

Let's look at Exodus 38:22-23, where we find the names of Bezalel and Aholiab. Bezalel #1212 meaning "in the shadow of God" "or protected of God." Aholiab #171 meaning "father's tent" or "of the father's tent."

Bezalel is mentioned in the Bible ten times and Aholiab is mentioned five times, not for the great wonders they did or the great feats of strength or miraculous victories, but for a job well done. For faithfully fulfilling their purpose God honors them in His book, the Bible, for over 3,000 years, just because they did a good job building His Tabernacle!!

Their names are recorded here in God's Word, our Rock. God honors them unto time immemorial, even though in Exodus

35:30 it says, "God called by name," He chose them, and He filled them with His Spirit, in wisdom, understanding and knowledge of all manner of workmanship, to build that Tabernacle and still God honors them, because they fulfilled their purpose. See, God does not necessarily choose only the qualified for His purposes, He qualifies who He chooses. Wow, then He honors them anyway, as if their name were written in stone and "Pekudei" numbered with the stars.

In Exodus 39:6-15, we read that the names of the twelve sons of Israel were engraved in stone, in onyx and set in gold on the shoulders of the Ephod as a memorial, and that the breastplate had four rows of three precious stones, each engraved with the name of one of the twelve tribes of Israel like a signet, each their own stone. Sardis, topaz and emerald, turquoise, sapphire and diamond, Jacinth, agate and amethyst, beryl, onyx and Jasper. Those names: Reuben, Simeon and Levi, Judah, Zebulun and Issachar, Dan, Gad and Asher, Naphtali, Benjamin and Joseph (Ephraim/Manasseh). Those names engraved in stone, are forever engraved on the hearts and in the minds of the Jewish people, recorded in the Bible as examples to us all. God's chosen, His people's names engraved in rock "Pekudei" numbered with the stars.

In Hebrew the word for rock is "tsur #6697" and is used as one of the many Names or titles describing God, Yahweh Tsur, the Lord my Rock. 1 Samuel 2:2 reads, "no one is Holy like the Lord, for there is none besides You, nor is there any Rock like our God."

Psalm 95:1 reads, "Come let's sing joyfully to Lord! Let us

make a joyful noise to the Rock of our salvation! Let us come into His presence with thanksgiving, and make a joyful noise to Him with pslams."

The Old Testament and New Testament both identify, God, Yahweh and Jesus, Yeshua as the Spiritual Rock that accompanied the children of Israel during their long journey through the wilderness, Yeshua is also the Stone which the builders rejected, but has become the Chief Cornerstone of God's Church (Psalm 118:22, Luke 20:17).

Exodus 40:34, records that when the Tabernacle "Mishkan #4908" was finished, God's presence filled the Tent with His Shekinah #7931. Now all who helped build the Tabernacle and Temple, be they renowned or unknown are "counted" as building stones and are "Pekudei," numbered with the stars. "You also, as living stones, are being built up a spiritual house, a holy priesthood, to offer up spiritual sacrifices acceptable to God through Jesus Christ" (1 Peter 2:5).

Think about that, you are "Pekudei" numbered, accounted for service, as stones in the Spiritual House, Mishkan of Yeshua Messiah. First Peter 2:9 goes on to say, "But you are a chosen generation, a royal priesthood, a holy nation, His own special people, that you may proclaim the praises of Him who called you out of darkness into His marvelous light."

Haftarah Portion
2 Kings 12:1-17

2 Kings 12:1-17 records the name of Jehoash the king, who

faithfully restores the Temple of the Lord. His purpose? Then only a few years later he gives all the sacred things from the House of the Lord to the invading king of Syria because he fell into apostasy after his godly counselor Jehoiada died. The invasion came as a judgment of his wickedness. Honor and infamy recorded in God's book forever, "Pekudei" numbered with the stars and like engraved in stone. Find your purpose and stay true to it (Ecclesiastes 3:1).

Gospel Portion
John 6:1-71

John chapter 6 records some of the miracles done by Jesus, Yeshua, He fed the 5,000 with just five loaves and two fishes, He walked on the water and here Jesus tells His followers that He is the "bread of life," "the hidden manna" (John 6:48), then in verse 53 Yeshua says, "most assuredly, I say to you, unless you eat of the flesh of the Son of Man and drink His blood, you have no life in you."

Yeshua, Jesus was teaching that only through faith in Him could a person be "Pekudei" numbered and have everlasting life. It was such a hard thing to understand at the time that many of His followers rejected Him to follow Him no more (John 6:66).

We all have been chosen of God, but we still have to choose to follow Him. John 6:70 says, "Jesus answered them, did I not choose you, the twelve, and one of you is a devil? He spoke of Judas Iscariot, the one who would betray Him." Twelve names: Simon Peter, Andrew, James, John, Philip,

From GOD through Moses to YOU

Bartholomew, Matthew, Thomas, James, Thaddaeus, Simon the Canaanite and Judas Iscariot the one who would betray Him. Eleven names, names of honor. One name of dishonor. All but one recorded in the Lamb's Book of life, as if engraved in stone (Revelation 20:3).

"He who has an ear, let him hear what the Spirit says to the churches. To him who overcomes I will give some of the hidden manna to eat and I will give him a white stone, and on that stone a new name written which no one knows except him who receives it." (Revelation 2:17)

Your new name engraved on a white stone, forever set in the breastplate of righteousness of the high priest of the order of Melch Tzedek #6664, Who is Yeshua Messiah, your name forever recorded in the Lamb's book of life, appointed for service "Pekudei," a name of honor before God, like it was engraved in precious stone. Amen.

Would you like to be "Pekudei" numbered, appointed for service unto the Lord? Would you like your name engraved on a precious white stone? Jesus has already chosen you, He waits for you to choose Him and it's easy as ABC.

A. Admit, it that you have sinned and ask forgiveness.
B. Believe, believe Jesus died for that sin, then rose from the grave three days later.
C. Confess, confess with your mouth that Jesus is Lord and make Him King in your life.

Read Romans 10:8-13 and John 3:16 then pray, repent and

ask God to fill you with His Holy Spirit and appoint you for service in His Kingdom asking in Jesus's Name. Amen.

If you prayed that prayer go tell a Pastor, a Messianic Rabbi or a Christian friend they will know what to do next. You can contact us here at jewandgentileministries.org

---

Bibliography for Pekudei "numbered"
Interlinear Bible, The Hendrickson publishing, 2006
New King James Version of the Bible, Thomas Nelson publishers, 2007
Strong's Complete Dictionary of the Bible Words, Thomas Nelson publishing, 1996

NOTES:

Glossary

Ab # 1 father-abba
Abat #5670 give generously
Able #1892 vapor
Abronah #5684 filled with wrath
Acharei Mot #310 and 4194 after the death
Adashah #5742 lentils
Adonijah #138 (Adonaiyyahu) my Lord is YHVH
Aholiab #171 fathers tent
Akal #784 consuming
Al #5921 upon, over
Almon Diblathaim #5963, 1690 hidden, fig cakes
Alush #442, crowd, tumult of men
Amen #539 (aman) believe, faith, trust
Amanah #548 faith, agreement, support
Amar #559 say, said, speak
Ani #589 myself, I, me
Ani #6041 humble, in need
Anikim (anaq, Anak) #6062 neck, giant people
Arba #702 four
Arche #746 beginning
Aron #727 Ark, chest
Asar #6237 one tenth
Asenath #621 belongs to neith
Avon #5771 iniquity, sin, guilt
Azab #5800 forsake

B'resheet #7225 in the beginning
Balaam #1109 pilgrim of, foreigner
Balak #1111 devastator, destroyer
Bamidbar #4057b wilderness
Beha'alotcha #5927 when you light
Bahar #2022 (Har) in mount or on mountain
Beer Sheba #875, 7651 seven wells
Bechukotai #2708 in my statutes
Bekorah #1062 birthright
Ben #1121 son
Bene Elohim #1121, 430 fallen Angels
Bene Jaakan #1142 sons of intelligence
Berith (Brit) #1285 covenant
Beshalach #7971 when sent
Bethabara #1012 house at the ford
Bethel #1008 house of God
Beulah #1166 married
Bezalel (Betsalel) #1212 in the shadow of
Bikkurim #1061 firstfruits
Bo #935 go

Caleb #3612 whole heart
Chadashah #2319 new
Chalam #2472 dream, dreamer
Charad #2730 fear, highly respect
Chatah #2398 to miss, go wrong
Chayei #2416 living
Chazaq #2388 arrogant, prideful
Chodesh #2320 month, moon
Chosheck #2822 darkness, obscurity

Glossary

Chukat #2708 statutes
Corban #2878 offering to God, a gift

Dabar #1697 speech, word, spoken
Derek #1869-70 (darak) way, walk, aim at, practice
Devarim #1677 words
Dibon Gad #1769, 1408 wasting of God
Dophkah #1850 driven

Ebed #5650 slave
Echad #259 one
Eduth #5715 testimony
Ekev #6118 because
El #410 God
El Bara #1254 Creator
Elim #362 Oaks
El Nasa #5375 God who forgives
Elohim #430 God
El Olam #5769 God everlasting
El Shaddai #7706b All Mighty
Emor #559 say, said, spoke
En #2258 (*Greek),* was
Eretz #776 earth, land
Erez #730 cedar
Esh #398 fire
Eshcol #6025 cluster (of grapes)
Etham #860 sea bound
Ev'en #1722 (*Greek),* in
Ezion Gebor #6100 giants backbone

Gaal #1350 redeemer (goel)

Gadol #1419 great

Gath #1661 press or vat

Geshem #1653 rain

Gethsemane #1068 *(Greek),* olive press

Goel #1350 (gaal) kinsman redeemer

Gomorrah #6017 deals violently

Gospel #2097 *(Greek),* good news

Goral #1486 cast lots

Goyim #1471 people, nations, gentiles

Gudgodah #1412 cleft

Ha'azinu #238 to give ear, listen

Hallelujah #239 *(Greek),* praise the Lord

Har #2022 mountain

Harah #2030 conceive

Haradah #2732 fear

Haran #2771 arid

Hashmonah #2832 fruitfulness

Hay #1887 behold, look

Hayah #1961 to become or am

Hazorth #2689 enclosures

Hebron #2275 city in S. Judah

Hephzibah #2656 my delight

Hittite #2850 terror

Hor Haggidgad cleft in the mountain

Hosanna #5614 *(Greek),* save we pray

Ichthus #2486 *(Greek),* fish

Ije Abrarim son #5856, 5682 ruins of Abraham

Imrah #565a. utter, speech, word

Immanuel #6005 *(Greek),* God with us

Isaac #3327 laughter
Ish #376 man, husband
Immarh #565 utterance, speech, word

Jairus #2971 (Yair) enlightener
Jedidiah #3041 beloved of Yah
Jephthah #3316 he opens
Jethro #3503 preeminence or his excellence
Jezreel #3157 God sows
Joshua #3091 God saves
Jot Bathah #3193 pleasantness
Jubilee (yobel) #3104 rams horn
Judah #3063 praise

Kachash #3584 denies
Kanaph #3671 wings
Kadesh (qodesh) #6943 sanctuary #6946 holy
Kapporeth #3727 mercy seat
Kedoshim #6944 holy people
Ki #3588 for, when
Kibroth Hattaavah #6613, 8378 the graves of lust
Kippur #3725 atonement
Kir #7023 wall
Kirjath Arba #7153 (Hebron) city of the four
Ki Tavo #935 when you come, go
Ki Tetze #3316 when you go out
Ki tov #3588, 2895 that's good
Kohen #3548 priest
Korach #7141 bald
Kumi #2891 (*Greek*), arise

L'anu #580 us, we
Lagos #3056 (*Greek*), word
Lech lecha #1980 go out, to go, walk
Lechem #3899 bread
Libnah #3841 white
Lo #3808 no, never

Makheloth #4722 assembly of peace
Malachi #4397 (malak) messenger, angel
Malaki #4401 messenger (same as prophet Malachi)
Marah #4751 bitter
Mashal #4910 ruler
Mashash #4959 feel, grope
Massai #4550 journey
Mattah #4924 Rod
Mattot #4294 tribes
Melech Olam #4430 and 5769 King Everlasting
Melek #4428 king and King
Menorah #4501 lampstand
Meod #3966 very
Meshach #4887 anointed with oil
Messiah #4899 anointed one
Metsudah #4686b fortress
Midol #4024 tower
Miqqedesh #4720 sacred place, holy place
Miketz #7093 at the end
Millu #4394 consecrate, fill your hand
Mishkan #4908 dwelling place, tabernacle
Mishpatim #4941 judgements
Mithkah #4989 sweetness

Mitzvah #4687 commandments
Mizbeakh #4196 altar
Moab #4124 from my father
Moriah #4179 mountain of sacrifice
Moses #4822 because I drew him out of the water
Moserah #4149 correction
M'qodesh #6942 holy title for YHVH
M'tzora #6879 leper

Naar #5288 young man
Nadar #5087 vow, oath
Nakeh #5223 exposed
Naqam #5359 vengeance
Nasa #5357 forgives
Nasso #5375 lift up
Nathanael #5417 given of God
Nazir #5139 Nazirite
Nebo #5015 hollow
Nephillim #5303 giants
Nes #5251 flag, banner
Ner #5216 lamp
Neum #5002 says, vows, declares
Nissai (Nes) #5251 banner
Noach #5146 (Noah) rest
Nitzavim #5234 standing
Nun #5125 increase, propagate

Oboth #88 desires
Omnuo #3660 (*Greek),* swear
Olam #5769 everlasting (olam haba the new world to come)

Paidion #3813 (*Greek*), child

Palat #6403 deliverer

Panim #6440 face

Pasach #6458 Passover

Parashah #6575, 6567 (parashat) portion, to make distinct

Pekudei #6485 numbered

Peniel #6439 face of God (Penuel)

Pinchas #6372 mouth of the serpent

Pisgah #6449 cleft

Poti Pherah #6319 Josephs father- in -law

Puah #6312 splendid one

Punon #6325 precious stone

Qanah #7065 jealous

Qara #7121 call

Qatsar #7114 harvest

Qhal #6950 assembled

Qo #6958 vomit, spew

Qodesh #6944 holy, sanctified #6943 Qedesh, kodesh

Qumi #6965 arise

Raah #7462a shepherd

Rapha #7495 to heal

Red Sea #5480 sea of reeds

Re'eh #2009 behold

Rephaim #7497b giants

Rephidim #7508 beds, expenses, stretches

Reshith #7225 beginning, firstfruits

Reuel #7467 friend of God

Rissah #7446 dew

Rithmah #7575 noise

Rimmon Perez #7428 pomegranates of wrath
Ruach #7307 Spirit, breath, blew

Sabbath #7673 rest
Sar #8268 prince
Sarah #8283 princess
Satan #7854 adversary
Shabba #7650 made covenant
Shaddai #7706b Almighty
Shakan #7931 dwell, inhabit, nest
Shalom #7965 complete, whole
Sham #8033 there
Shama (Shamah) #8085 here
Shamar #8104 to keep, preserve, watch
Shamayim #8064 heaven(s), sky
Shaphat #8199 judge
Shaqed #8245, 46 Almond, the awakener
Sharath #8334 minister, aide
Shavuot #7620 feast of weeks
Shelach #7971 to send
Shemot #8034 names
Shepher #8234 beauty
Shiphrah #8036 beautiful one
Sh'mini #8066 eighth
Shoftim #8199 judges
Shophar #7782 a horn trumpet
Shub #7725 repent, returns
Shulchan #7979 table
Shuvua (Shabua) #7620 seven, week
Solomon #8010 (Shelomoh) too complete (from 7999)

Sukkot #5521 Feast of Tabernacles
Sullam #5551 ladder, staircase, highway

Tahath #8480 instead of
Tallit #2926 prayer shawl
Tamim #8549 perfect, unspotted, unblemished
Tazera #2232 sow, scatter seed, conceive
Tehillah #8416 song of praise (tehillim-psalm)
Terah #8646 turning, duration
Terumah #8641 offering, contribution
Tetzaveh #6680 command
Theoreo #2334 (*Greek*), seeing
Tirosh #8492 juice, new wine
Toldot #8425 generations
Torah #8451 instruction
Tsabaoth #6635 hosts, army
Tsadoq #6659 (Zadok), righteous
Tsedeq #6664 righteous
Tselem #6754 likeness
Tsit tsit #6731 tassels
Tsmach #6780 branch
Tsur #6697 rock
Tzav #6680 command

Va'era #7200 and I appeared
Va et chanan #2603 and I implored
Vayalech #3212 and went, same as #1980 halech
Vaya'qhal #6950 and assembled
Vayechi #2416 and he lived
Vayeshev #376 and 3427 and he dwelt
Vayetze #3318 went out

Vayigash #5066 and he appeared
Vayikra #7121 and he called
Vayishlach #376 and 7971 and he sent (gave over)
Vazot Habracha #2008 and 1293 this is the blessing

Yadah #3034 confesses
Yarah #3384 throw, cast
Yathar #3498 have preeminence
Yehovah (Jehovah) #3068 Lord
Yeshav (yashab) #3427 dwell, inhabit
Yeshua #3444 salvation
YHVH #3068 Lord
Yithrah #3502 abundance, riches
Yitro #3503 (Jethro) Moses father- in- law
Yirah #7200 provide, see a need
Yobal #3104 jubilee
Yom #3117 day

Zahab #2091 gold
Zalmonah #6758 shade
Zamar #2167 play instruments in praise
Zaphnath-paaneah #6847 the god speaks and lives
Zebech #2077 slaughter for sacrifice
Zechariah #2148 Yah has remembered
Zekar #2142 title, memorial name
Zur #2114 strange, unusual

Would you like to learn more about
Hebraic roots and Messianic ways?
Read this very interesting and enlightening
book about Dr. Karen Y. Ranney's exciting
and joy filled journey learning about God's
Plan for Jew and Gentile alike.